In Light & Love

My Guide to Balance

"In Light & Love" Series - Book 1

Lisa Gornall

Copyright © 2013, 2014 Lisa Gornall

All rights reserved. In accordance with the U.S. Copyright Act of 1976, the scanning, uploading, and electronic sharing of any part of this book without the permission of the publisher is unlawful piracy and theft of the author's intellectual property.

This work is solely for personal growth, education, and recreation. It is not a therapeutic activity, such as psychotherapy, counseling, or medical advice, and it should not be treated as a substitute for any professional assistance. In the event of physical or mental distress, please consult with appropriate professionals. The application of protocols and information in this book is the choice of each reader, who assumes full responsibility for his or her understandings, interpretations, and results. The author and the publisher assume no responsibility for the actions or choices of any reader.

Contents

1 - Foreword 1

Beginning to Live Consciously 2

How to Use this Book 3

2 - Starting Your Journey 5

What is White Light 6

How to Bring in White Light 6

Using Your Intuition 8

3 - Becoming Aware of Your Energy 12

Thoughts and Words Create Your Reality 12

Be Aware of the Words you Use 12

The Power of Your Mind 14

4 - Letting Go 16

Why it is Important to Let Go 16

Why We Have Experiences 18

Creating a Safe Space 18

Letting Go 19

Always Be Objective 20

Your Body is Your Guide 22

Letting Go Exercises 22

Mini Letting Go Sessions to Get Back into Balance Right Away 33

When is My Session Done? 36

Struggling with Your "I am" Statement 36

Supporting Your Body 37

Appreciating Yourself and Your Process 38

The Waiting Place 38

Releasing an Energy 43

Overview 55

5 - Living in Balance with Others 57

Becoming Energy Conscious 57

Feel Safe without Building Walls 62

Changing Your Dance with Others 63

Being Aware of Your Energy in a Conflict 65

Creating Peace in Relationships from Long Ago 68

6 - Living in Balance From Within 71

Be Aware of Your Energy Level 72

Learning to Find Your Balance 74

Regaining Balance 76

Meditation 78

Mini Meditations 80

Color Meditations 81

Meditation to Heal the Earth 84

7 - We Are All One 88

A Ball of White Light 88

Karma 89

Remembering We Are Love, We Are One 92

8 - Tips to Balance Your Body, Mind, and Spirit 94

Tips for the Body 94

Tips for the Mind 100

Tips to Connect with Your Spirit 107

9 - As You Go on Your Journey 115

Acknowledgments

To my daughters Emily and Megan. Thank you for helping me to learn balance in every moment no matter what craziness was happening around us.

1 - Foreword

At some point, you get settled in your career, family, and friendships and you forget that life is all about change. The seasons change, your environment changes, and people change. Children grow and your body ages, no matter how you may try to fight it.

Often, you reach a point in your life where not living consciously (being aware of your actions, choices, and the impact of these on the whole Universe), is no longer an option. No matter how you may fight to keep things as they are, you are being pushed to live consciously.

You may reach this awareness or "ah hah" moment through an illness, losing a loved one, a major life change, or losing a job. Somehow, something happens to you in a dramatic way to get you back on track and living consciously.

Just like aging, you may fight this inevitable change in your life. You may feel stuck and trapped with fear. This fear of changing, the unknown, is what paralyzes you, the actual change frees you.

You may also be afraid of the changes that are going to happen and the things you think you will not have control over. Here are some tips to help you move past this fear:

* You did not have control before when you were living subconsciously, it was an illusion. It was as if you were

driving your car with your eyes closed. You were gripping the steering wheel tightly with clenched fists afraid of what was around the next corner.

* Life is so much easier when you live consciously. You will see that you are driving your car with your eyes open, aware of your surroundings and actions, and you are fully supported.

* Being afraid to make these changes in your life is the hardest part of your journey, not the change itself. The key is to let go of the fear that is holding you trapped, stuck, or frozen. That fear is what is controlling you in this moment. Do not worry; there are sections in this book to help you with this.

You may not have complete control of what is happening around you, but you can control how you respond to it. Your thoughts and actions in this moment create your reality. Balance is possible in every moment.

Beginning to Live Consciously

Once you begin your journey to live consciously, you will find that it will also have a significant impact on those around you.

You will find that the people you once considered close friends may now seem so different from you that the friendship will fade or disappear altogether.

Friends that have no interest in living consciously may try to keep pulling you back out of balance. Perhaps they can only be friends if that dysfunction is in your relationship. They will try to keep you in the type of friendship you have had together because that is what they know. They may not be comfortable with anything else.

That is okay, because at this point, you will start attracting people to you that are similar. They are like-minded and they prefer to live in balance rather than chaos. They appreciate the journey you are on because they have experienced it or they are experiencing it now.

You will find that you are much happier living consciously, but it will be different at first. In the beginning, it can seem overwhelming, especially without a guide to help you through it. I have been where you are and I have helped many people find their balance and get back on track.

You are living in a fast-paced world. You no longer have to go through a long, drawn-out-philosophical process to experience God, love, the Universe, White Light, spirituality, or whatever you would like to call it. The tools in this book will help you connect and find your balance easily and quickly.

How to Use this Book

As you go through this book, turn to the sections that will help you restore your balance with your body, mind, and spirit, in any given moment. Practice what you read. Read a section and apply it to your life in that moment. If you are feeling out of balance; sit down, find the sections of this book that apply to you in that moment, and apply them to your life for at least a few days.

This book is full of the tools that I use when working with my clients. The work I do is completely intuitive. I know why a client is holding energy in a certain place and how they can let it go to get back into balance in that moment.

Every situation is different. What works in this moment may require a tweak to work a few minutes later. Trust your intuition (what you are getting to do, your immediate insight), to help yourself in any given moment. I have written this book to provide examples that you can apply in your own life. It is here to help you find balance no matter what challenges you are facing.

You will see that balance is possible in every moment and that your life is so much easier when you are in balance. Use the tools in this book to create your routines and practices to live in light and balance.

In Light and Love,

Lisa

2 - Starting Your Journey

Life is a process where you learn balance. When you get out of balance (and it can happen so easily), everything seems to fall apart. There are many simple things you can do to help get yourself back into balance. It all begins with reconnecting with your truth:

I am love. I am light. We are all one.

This is truth. You know this to be true; you can feel it inside of you when you say those words. They feel peaceful and freeing.

This is often forgotten in our day-to-day routine. Somehow the darkness creeps in. Whether it is the anger and frustration we pick up throughout the day and store in our bodies to deal with later (and then we forget), the thoughts that are judging us and others, negativity in our surroundings, or the darkness that sometimes appears to swallow you in, these are not truth. They are simply the absence of love. Negativity or darkness has no power unless we give it power. It is an illusion or a shadow that disappears quickly when we remember the truth; only love is real.

This can seem like a juggling act, where up until this point, any darkness has had an illusion of much power. However there is a shift happening. We are no longer okay with the negativity and we are receiving daily confirmations we are on the right track when we focus on love and light.

Love is light. Love conquers all. The moment we remember

that, we reclaim our power and the darkness goes away.

What is White Light

You are a being of love. Visually, it is seen as a White Light shining through and around you.

In pictures of spiritual people, the White Light is drawn around their bodies. This White Light is not reserved for "some" people. We are all made of White Light. We are all connected by the White Light. The White Light is in you. The White Light is love.

White Light is God, love, the Universe, really you can call it what you like. It is non-denominational; it simply is. It is what we are.

We are love, we are light. It feels nurturing and supportive because it is. Before we inhabit our bodies, love is all we know. This is our truth and we can return to it at any moment.

How to Bring in White Light

Being that we are light, it is very easy to bring it into your body. The White Light helps you feel calm, centered, and balanced. Imagine the White Light you see shining through trees or through clouds over lakes or oceans.

When you bring the White Light through your body you can be standing, sitting, or lying down. Choose what is the most comfortable for you in this moment (although if you lay down, you may fall asleep). Just make sure you do not cross your arms, legs, or feet as that will slow the energy down.

Now it is time for you to try it. Imagine the White Light and let it flow through each part of your body.

Close your eyes. Imagine that White Light shining down on you. The White Light comes in through the top of your crown (top of your head), down your face, your neck, into your shoulders, down your chest and back, into your stomach, into your hips, down into your thighs, to your knees, down your legs, and into your feet. The White Light flows from the center of your feet, down into the Earth. You become one with the light and the light flows into you and into the Earth. You will feel calm, centered, and at peace. You will be grounded.

If you feel tension, simply take a deep breath of White Light and imagine pushing the tension out of your body. If it is difficult to push out, that is okay. That just means there is some letting go to do in that area. (See the Letting Go section, Chapter 4.)

Practice bringing the White Light in at least once a day for five minutes. When this becomes a part of your routine, practice bringing it in twice a day for at least five minutes. The goal is to eventually do it throughout the day as your body gets out of balance and whenever you feel your body can use some White Light.

If you find yourself having a hard time visualizing the light, you can stand outside under the sun or under a light. You can also use your hands to help bring the White Light through your body. Just bring your hands up in the air over your head and slowly bring them down your body (without touching your body), until you bring the White Light through your feet and into the Earth.

If you feel like you are floating in the air or you feel spacey, bring the White Light through your body again and make sure it goes through your feet and into the Earth. This will help ground you. It may seem fun to feel like you are floating, but this takes a lot of energy and you will not make the best decisions unless you are grounded.

Using Your Intuition
Intuition and the Mind

Intuition is not something that your mind can make up. The mind is not that creative. The mind really questions things, ponders validity, and likes to have order (everything has a place.) Intuition is possibilities without limitation. Often, we dismiss our intuition because our mind cannot make sense of it or we do not trust our intuition.

Intuition can be a feeling or a sense of something coming (often called your gut feeling). It can be something you see happening soon or in the future. Perhaps, it is something you just "know" without any logic or reasoning. Intuition can also be something you hear. Everyone experiences their intuition in different ways. How do you experience yours?

Trusting

Trusting your intuition is something that usually happens over time. You will have a feeling, sense something, know something, and it happens. The first time it may seem like a coincidence (which there is no such thing), but after a few times, you will start to trust what you are getting, seeing, sensing. Just remember, it is not something that has to be proven to your mind or anyone else's. Sometimes it cannot be. Sometimes it can. The point is that your intuition is here to help you, to guide you, to support you.

One thing to know about intuition is that things change CONSTANTLY, especially when you are going with the flow. Just because you are getting that this is the way to do something right now, or that something is going to happen a specific way does not mean it will. There are so many other things in place, so many free wills. This by no means is a sign that your intuition is not working. Things change. Life is full of change. Sometimes we see something that takes years to happen.

Use your intuition as your guide. Whatever intuition you are getting in a moment, it is true. The question then becomes, am I supposed to do something with this? If you are, then do what you are being guided to do. If not, it may be something to help you know you are on track, or it might be something for you to know and do something with at a later time.

Whatever your intuition tells you, it is important to let it go, do not hold onto it. Everything happens as it should. Everything always works out in the most perfect way possible. Life flows, just like energy, just like our intuition.

Creating Your Reality

The most powerful words you can say to the Universe are *"I AM,"* and believe it.

"I am love. I am safe. I am whole. I am supported by the Universe. I am _____."

I am means that you already are. The words you say to the Universe become your reality. I often use several "I am" statements at a time for myself and when working with clients. The ones I find people use the most in the beginning are:

* I am Love.
* I am Light.
* I am Safe.
* I am Whole.
* I am Peace.
* I am One with the Universe, or I am supported by the Universe.

When you are introducing a new "I am" statement, make sure you start off by bringing the White Light through your body. Let the White Light radiate through every part of you. Then say, "I am _____."

Notice where you are resisting your, "I am _____." This is an area where letting go is to be done.

When you release the resistance, the "I am" will easily replace whatever was there originally. Sometimes it is helpful to use another "I am" statement with the one you are trying to connect with.

My "I am" Statement is not Working

You have to believe what you say. If you do not believe it, you cannot say, "I am peace" when you feel completely irritated. The parts of you that are irritated are screaming at you, "No, I am not peace and you cannot pretend I am!!!" Notice the, "you cannot pretend I am." Your body knows you cannot pretend and so do the beliefs that are hiding. The goal is not to pretend. The goal is to KNOW, "I am peace," as your new reality.

Start by letting go of whatever is making you feel irritated. Bring the White Light through, imagine the irritation floating away like smoke and then fill the space where that irritation was with some supportive "I am." "I am love. I am light. I am peace." This is a process that will lead to the original "I am" statement, "I am peace." Keep doing this until you can connect with your "I am" statement.

3 - Becoming Aware of Your Energy

Every thought you think and every word you use creates your reality. As you have heard, like attracts like.

If you are thinking positive, loving thoughts, you will attract more of those thoughts and that will become your reality. However, if you are thinking negative thoughts and you are judging yourself, you will attract more negativity and this will be your reality. It is easy to get stuck in the negativity, especially when there is always a villain, bad guy, or scapegoat in our society. This does not have to be your reality, you have a choice.

What are you thinking? What are you saying? What reality are you creating for yourself?

Thoughts and Words Create Your Reality

Every thought you think and every word you use creates your reality in this moment. This moment then shapes the next moment, and so on. Things are put into motion and become reality without you consciously being aware of what you put into motion. What does this mean? It means that your thoughts and your words are very powerful even if you are not aware of what you are thinking and saying. Pay attention to them!

Be Aware of the Words you Use

Imagine that the Universe is a server in a restaurant and your mind orders from the server what it would like to have. The moment you think a thought, you order it. The server brings it to you. The Universe always brings you what you ask for. If you say, "I cannot do this," "I am not good enough," "I do not deserve to have money," this becomes your reality. Now mentally erase all of these statements as this is not what we are going to create.

Really think about the words you are using and the thoughts you are creating because this becomes your reality.

The words you use mean what they say. For example, if you say you "need" something, you are right. You are going to keep on needing it for a long time. Same thing with want, desire, wish. They are words we use every day in our society without giving them a second thought and we give these words much power. There are other words you can use to replace them; it just takes some thinking on your part (it is always good to think before you speak.) For example, instead of, "I need to eat," you can say, "It is time for me to eat," or "my stomach is hungry."

Practice replacing the words: need, want, desire, wish, crave with other words the moment you use them. Do not get discouraged. Remember, you have been using these words for a long time, it does not have to take a long time to change your vocabulary, but chances are, you will be practicing this for a couple of weeks.

The Power of Your Mind

Our minds are often filled with negative thoughts a majority of the day. Since most of the talking we do is to ourselves, you can see where this can lead to creating realities we are not even aware of creating. Stopping negative thoughts when they come up gets easier the more you do it.

To stop the thought you can imagine the following:

* A red stop sign stopping the thought immediately
* A red stop light that forces the thought to come to a screeching halt
* Putting the thought on ice and freezing it
* Slamming the brakes on the thought

Find what works for you. You may use different ways for different thoughts.

Immediately, you replace it with being grateful for something. It can be anything, but it has to be something that you are thankful for in that moment.

Being grateful is the most powerful thing you can do. It immediately puts you into the present moment and allows more things you are grateful for to be present.

You can be grateful for anything such as:

* Being able to take a breath
* Your family
* Your friends
* Your job

* The seat in which you are sitting
* The smells in the air
* The abundance surrounding you
* Be grateful for anything at that moment that pops into your mind when you close your eyes.

Try it now. Really appreciate what you are grateful for in this moment. "I am grateful for_____."

Being appreciative attracts even MORE positive things into our lives as like attracts like. Remember, if you are thinking negative thoughts, you will attract more negative thoughts. If you change your negative thought and focus on something positive, you will attract more positive things into your life at that moment.

The moment you think of something you are grateful for, you are filled with appreciation and that becomes your reality. Since this moment shapes your next, you will start attracting more things you are grateful for into your life.

4 - Letting Go

Why it is Important to Let Go

Letting go is a process you can use to help release the tension, worry, frustration, old beliefs, and old energy you store in your body. As a society, we are taught to deal with stuff later. As the day ends, the week ends, the month ends, you often forget about it. You bury it and forget about it until you are forced to deal with it.

Pay attention and notice as you go through your day where you store tension, frustration, stress, and irritation all with the intent of dealing with it later. You can also ask yourself right now, "Where do I store my energy?" This will tell you some places you can begin letting go.

Just because you are not paying attention to the energy, does not mean it is not there. Often, you will notice the energy when your body literally cannot take the buildup anymore and you start feeling it in a physical form. Maybe you feel like you are having a hard time breathing, or your stomach hurts, or you feel like your legs are really stiff (and you did not just finish an intense workout). This is your body's way of telling you something is not right so pay attention to this area.

You may also notice darkness or dark smoke as you are bringing the White Light through your body. This is also a sign that this area in your body is holding onto energy that is ready to be released.

Sometimes you will know exactly what you have to let go of in this moment. However, it is not necessary to always know what you are letting go of. As you start letting go, you will find that you know what your body is ready to release. Sometimes it will be a whole bunch of random things, sometimes a bunch of things that are all connected, and sometimes it may just be one big thing for you.

Over time, you will be able to do mini letting go sessions, whenever you would like to do one, wherever you are. Mini letting go sessions are for in the moment when you realize that you are holding onto "stuff" that just happened. They are done in the moment when you are not able to do a typical letting go session, or for when a little release will help you get into balance right away, like at work.

When you are letting go, you will release anything that no longer represents:

* Who you are
* Who you would like to be
* What you would like to be doing
* What you would like to be experiencing

Letting go creates balance. It shifts the focus of our energy off the past so we can be present in this moment. If your energy is stuck in the past, you will feel stuck and trapped, like you are not moving forward.

In the present moment is where you have power. This is where you create your next moment. When you let go, you are not completely going to forget what happened. You will remember the experience but without the baggage that weighs you down.

Why We Have Experiences

We have experiences so we can learn from them. There is no such thing as a mistake. Everything happens for a reason. Everything has a purpose. Sometimes this takes time to see, but you will eventually understand it all when the time is right and it will all make sense.

Creating a Safe Space

The first thing you always do before letting go is create a safe space.

The first time you do letting go on your own, do it somewhere you feel safe and at peace. This can be a space in your house, a space you like to go to and think, somewhere in nature, or somewhere that feels comfortable to you when you are getting ready to start.

"I am" statements also help you create a safe place to do your letting go throughout your process.

An "I am" statement that people use regardless of what they are letting go of is, "I am love." Whatever we are letting go of, it is important for us to remember that we are love. Not loved, but love, there is a difference in the meaning of these words and at this point, it is important to remember that you are love.

Other "I am" statements people use are "I am safe, I am whole, I am supported by the Universe, I am light."

Use whatever "I am" statement you feel most connected with. You can use one, or you can use several. Always start letting go by saying an "I am" statement.

For example, you can start with "I am love." Then as you go through and do some letting go, you will fill the space that you are clearing with this same "I am" statement. After you are done letting go for the moment, you will continue to use that "I am" statement for a few days. This will help you keep yourself in a safe space and fill the space you just cleared with the "I am" you are putting in that space.

For example: "I am love. I am safe. I am whole." I say this as I bring White Light through my body. I do my letting go (see the Letting Go Exercises), and I release that energy in my chest, stomach, leg (wherever it may be). I then put my "I am" mantra into that space. I no longer am full of whatever I was letting go of. I am now full of love, I am safe, and I am whole instead.

Where is your safe space?

What is your "I am" statement to help you feel safe while you are letting go today?

Letting Go

Letting go is like an onion. There are many layers and some

layers make you cry more than others.

Every letting go session is different. Even if you are working on a similar topic, what you are releasing now is different than what you released last time.

Trust yourself as you always know what to do and when to do it. The best time to release is when you have realized that there is letting go to do. This will become easier with time.

Often, you will find that what you are releasing are beliefs that you did not create for yourself. They are usually things you were told about life or yourself. You carry not only stuff from this life, but from all your lives. Since we live many lives and everything is connected (see the We Are All One section), what you release now affects your other lives as well. You may or may not be able to tell this is happening, but know that it is.

Always Be Objective

You have a perspective, a mental view, or an outlook on life. It is the way you have been taught to see the world through past experiences.

It is important to be objective when you are letting go. By being objective, it allows you to clearly see the fears, beliefs, expectations, and baggage you carry with you in any given situation. This allows you then to act in a different way and to let go of the things that no longer represent who you are.

Notice if your perspective and beliefs are still true for you in a situation?

Are these ways of seeing the world rooted in your family's perspective? Perhaps they are from another life and a totally different experience?

Often you will find that you act on beliefs you learned while growing up, but that belief does not fit your current situation anymore. Replace the old beliefs with something that is true for you now. For example: "Love is all there is," or "there is plenty for everyone including me."

What is true for you?

In some situations it helps to look at things in a different way, through a different perspective in order to have more clarity. This is especially helpful when you are letting go of something or if you are in an emotionally charged situation.

Looking at something objectively means that you look at the situation like it is not happening to you. It is as if whatever is happening does not directly affect you. You could pretend it is on TV or it is happening to someone else.

When you are first learning to look at things objectively, it is helpful to talk to other people about the situation. By doing this, you will see how other people would respond and it helps you to see other possible outcomes.

The purpose in being objective is to respond in the best way to a situation instead of shutting down or responding out of fear. When this happens, nothing is resolved.

Being objective gives you a way to choose how you think about yourself and the world, and how you respond.

Your Body is Your Guide

Your body will tell you where the energy is that you are ready to release. Become aware of any tension or stress you may be feeling anywhere in your body.

Notice where you are feeling:

* Stiffness
* Tension
* Frozen
* Where you see darkness or smoke when you bring the White Light through

Are you tensing your fingers into a fist? Are you holding your stomach? Are you getting a headache? Do you feel the weight of the world on your shoulders? Are you putting up a wall to protect yourself from everything good and bad?

Any of these places you answer yes is a place ready to let go. Start with the part of your body that is calling you the loudest. This will be the place that hurts the most or is causing you the most trouble. Then you can move on to the other places. Often you will find that they are all connected. Once you start to release one, the other areas will start to follow.

Letting Go Exercises

When I am helping someone through the letting go process, I

am reading their energy and using my intuition. I can feel the pain in my body. I will ask the client questions to help reduce the pain in my own body, and for them to become more aware of it in theirs. I know we are on track when the pain lessens in my body.

Sometimes, the pain will be stirred up again by another event, and we will go back to the pain again. Letting go is a process, just like everything else. The more you practice doing it, the easier it gets, and the more in tune you become with your body, mind, and spirit.

Begin by looking at yourself objectively in emotional situations. Notice when you start to feel a strong emotion. Then notice how you react physically. Ask yourself if this is how you would like to respond to this situation? If you answer no, there is letting go to be done. How would you like to react in this situation? What belief is keeping you from reacting the way you would like to?

Body Awareness Exercise
In this letting go process, your body is your guide. If you are feeling pain or tension anywhere, this is a good letting go process to use first.

1 - Start in a calm, safe, setting and pick some "I am" statements that make you feel safe and supported.

Bring the White Light through your body starting with the top (crown) of your head, through your body, and bring the White

Light into the center of your feet, and into the Earth.

"I am _____." Use your "I am" statement(s) through this process as often as you would like.

Notice how your body is feeling:

Do you feel your legs or your feet? (If you answer yes go to number three.)

Is there a part of you that you are ignoring or blocking? (If you answer yes go to number two.)

2 - If you do not feel connected with yourself (you cannot feel all of your body), bring the White Light through again. Use your hands to help guide the energy flowing through your body. You can also stand in the sunlight or under a light. "I am _____."

What can you do in this moment to have all of your body present? Perhaps you can imagine your body aligning? Would it help you to spend a few minutes seeing what is keeping you from connecting? (Is your mind somewhere else? Are you afraid to let go?) Would meditating help you connect with yourself? Maybe it would help if you stretch, walk around the room, wiggle your body around, or even run in place? Do whatever is popping into your mind to help you feel connected to your body and present in this moment. If nothing is standing out to you, see if there are any images or words that you are drawn to or that describe how you are feeling about what it is that you are letting go of.

If you are having a hard time connecting with yourself, you may seek the council of an energy healer to help you with the energy component of the letting go process. There are many people that can see where your energy is blocked and they may be able to help you do this letting go if you are unsure how to do it yourself. Energy healers are in many different specialties such as Reiki, therapeutic massage, Energy Coaches, and many more. You can find someone you feel comfortable with to help you start your process.

3 - Once you are connected and grounded, you are ready to begin. If you know exactly what you would like to let go of, you can start here and see where this energy is in your body.

If you do not know what exactly you are letting go of, you can start with what you feel in your body. Where is the tension, stress, or negativity at in your body? (Hips, knees, legs, stomach, chest, head, etc.) How does the tension, stress, or negativity feel in your body? (Some examples are: throbbing, churning, aching, stabbing, pounding, etc.) Where does this feeling from above come from? Can you link or connect this feeling to an image or an event in your life? If you cannot link the feeling to anything, that is okay. Sometimes you can release without knowing all the details of what you are releasing. Perhaps it is not important what you are releasing, your body is just ready to release it.

Usually you will know what you are releasing, where, and why. To help you discover where this came from:

* Where were you when you first experienced this feeling in your body?

* What was happening around you?
* How did the event that was happening make you feel?
* Did you store this energy anywhere else in your body?

What can you do to let go of this feeling in your body? What activity comes to your mind? Maybe writing it down on paper and tearing it up, or going for a jog. Look at some letting go exercises (see the next four sections), if you would like some suggestions. Feel free to adapt the exercise to you and this letting go experience.

The goal is to remove the tension or stress from your body. Imagine sending that energy up into the sky or the Universe. Remember, the Universe is love and only love. The Universe will turn the energy into love and it will disappear. This will not hurt the Universe in any way.

After you have done the above exercises, check back in with yourself. Are you feeling tension or stress anywhere else in your body from this event, and if so where is it? (If you answered yes, repeat the above exercise, starting at number one. If you answered no, go to step number four.)

4 - At this step in the process, you should be feeling peace and calm in your body. Now that you have let go of the stress or tension in your body, it is time to fill it with positive energy. Appreciate yourself for the experience that you had and whatever you learned from it. (Every experience has a purpose.) Create an "I am" statement for yourself that reflects how you are feeling in this

moment and put it somewhere that you can see it. For example: "I am safe, I am peace, I am love, I am whole, I am light." Write down your "I am_____," and whatever affirmations you are inspired to write at this moment as a support for you for the next few days.

Affirmation examples: "Everything works out perfectly for everyone involved;" "I surround my family in love;" "one small step a day will help me reach my goal." Decorate it with color or designs if you would like. Put it somewhere where you will see it often and be reminded of your affirmation. Make copies if you would like it in several places. Keep it until you no longer feel a pull to look at it and then recycle it.

5 - Appreciate yourself for the steps you have taken on your journey. "I am grateful for _____."

6 - Pamper yourself. How can you support and take care of your body at this moment? Remember, letting go takes a lot of energy so it is important to pamper yourself after a session. You can: sit in a comfy place, go to a park or beach, take a shower, go for a walk, light candles, or eat something your body is craving to support it. Do whatever feels pampering and nurturing to you at this moment.

Writing Exercise

This is a good way to do your first letting go session on your own if you have not done any type of energy work before.

1 - Go to your safe place. Bring the White Light through your

crown, through your body, into your feet, and into the Earth.

"I am _____."

2 - Write down on a piece of paper each idea, belief, criticism that you have heard, thought, and believed, and any "bad" experiences because of it, and cry, be angry, feel it all over again! This will help you let go of these beliefs that you have been holding for years. You can draw circles, lines, tree branches, or whatever you would like on the paper first. You can write on post it notes, paper, facial tissue, toilet paper, rocks, leaves, whatever and wherever you are inspired to write these beliefs on. (Note: you will be getting rid of whatever you write it on as part of the releasing.)

3 - The next step is to physically get rid of the writings. You will look at each thing you wrote down and you will tear it off (if you can). Release the energy to the Universe.

Then you will appreciate that you had that experience. "From this experience, I learned_____."

You can dispose of the ideas by tearing them up, crinkling them up, putting each individual one in the paper shredder, flushing it down the toilet (if you used toilet paper), by burning them in a fireplace or fire pit (if this is safe to do), or you can put all the paper in a big bowl of water, or maybe the tub and swirl it around with your hands before putting it into the trash (outside your home, you do not want to keep thinking about it sitting in your kitchen or your office trash. Put it somewhere that once it is there, you do not have to move it again out of your house.) Then say your "I am" statement(s). "I am _____."

Imagine that you are consciously getting rid of the energy in your body as you get rid of each item you wrote on. Bring the White Light through and say your "I am" statements as often as you would like. Consciously you are removing the ideas out of your body and cleaning your body of these beliefs. For good measure, you are disposing of it all however you see fit. If you are using water to dispose of the writings, imagine you are washing the ideas out of your body. If you burn the paper in your fireplace, you are burning the ideas up and out of your body. If you are tearing up the paper, you are ripping it out of your body.

4 - Appreciate! Appreciate yourself for this whole process. Appreciate the experience that the beliefs gave you. Appreciate that you are now ready for positive energy and that you are ready to move forward, fill your body with your "I am _____."

5 - Start celebrating! Try doing something simple and FUN. It does not have to take a lot of time. Maybe dance your way through the house, wear something different or something that pampers your body, or treat yourself to something you think is special. Do anything that is fun to you and appreciate that you are moving forward!

If you are always celebrating with other people, try to make this celebration special by doing it by yourself. And vice versa, if you celebrate alone typically, celebrate this with other people. Celebration is important. It ends one cycle and shows the start of another. Without celebration, it seems there is no beginning and no end. Just a constant go, go, go. It is important to pause and appreciate the work you do.

Visualizing Exercise

You can visualize moving the energy. If you have done energy work, you may feel more comfortable starting with this approach.

1 - Go to your safe place. Bring the White Light through your crown, through your body, into your feet, and into the Earth.

"I am _____."

2 - Notice where there is darkness, tension, or gray smoke in your body. Start with the area that is calling your attention the most.

Imagine sending that energy up into the sky or the Universe (the Universe is all love. The Universe will turn the energy into love and it will disappear.)

You can imagine pulling the energy out like a weed. It can flow out like smoke. Whatever you see and feels right in that moment, do.

Bring the White Light and, "I am _____," in as often as you would like. Sometimes it helps to wiggle or shake that body part or move your body around.

3 - When it feels like it is gone, bring the White Light through your body again. "I am _____."

Does it still feel gone?

No? Keep going for as long as you can. Remember to stay in balance with your body. If you are feeling that your body has done all it can right now, do more another day.

4 - Is there more releasing to do somewhere else?

If you answer yes, release that energy if you can at this moment.

Remember to appreciate the experiences you have had, use your affirmations, and remember to celebrate!

Leaf Exercise

This is fun to do outside in nature. You can replace the leaf with sticks, rocks (if you have a stream or ocean to throw them into), or anything in nature that you would like to use.

1 - Go to your safe place. Bring the White Light through your crown, through your body, into your feet, and into the Earth.

"I am _____." Then write down any and all beliefs that are "bothering" you on an old leaf.

Group similar feelings/beliefs/thoughts together into piles.

2 - Pick up a section and start with the first leaf. Imagine the feeling/belief/thought leaving you as you start to crinkle the leaf. You can also let the leaf float into a river, creek, ocean, or lake. Remember to appreciate the experience and, "I am _____."

3 - As the leaf disappears, imagine any last traces of those beliefs disappearing with the leaf.

4 - When the leaves are gone or you no longer need to watch them disappear, say your, "I am _____." Appreciate yourself and the knowledge you have gained because of this experience.

5 - Pamper yourself. Do something fun for yourself, and celebrate!

Bath Tub Exercise

This is a good approach to use if you are feeling a pull to be in water. Water is a great resource when you are doing any letting go sessions. Sometimes people like to put their whole bodies in water, or sometimes just their feet, or up to their knees. Do what is best for you at this time.

1 - Light candles and safely put them around your bath tub. Fill your bath with things that are relaxing and pleasant to you: bubbles, bath salts, or relaxing music. Create your safe space. Bring the White Light through your crown, through your body, into your feet, and into the Earth. "I am _____."

2 - Once you are in the tub surrounded by the candles, look at what you are experiencing objectively, as if it were on TV, at the movies, or someone else's experience.

3 - Relax and let each feeling/belief/thought come into your mind. Let each belief go by blowing out a candle or popping a bubble. Group beliefs together.

For example: any beliefs about your body and its role in this experience for one candle, any beliefs about what you think about yourself during this experience for a different candle, etc. As you blow out the candle, imagine that you are taking the energy out of that belief. It no longer exists! You can imagine the energy going down the drain.

4 - When you are finished blowing out candles, drain the water out of the tub. As the tub is emptying, imagine any tension you are feeling in your body going down the drain. Rinse the tub and any remaining negativity away.

5 - Take a shower to rinse your body and any final tension down the drain. Imagine the shower water as the new energy flowing through and around your body. Appreciate yourself and this experience. "I am _____."

6 - Celebrate and pamper yourself. Do something fun for yourself. Sit in a warm comfy spot and drink something warm, eat a special treat, read a book, watch a favorite movie, or whatever you would like to do as a celebration in this moment.

Mini Letting Go Sessions to Get Back into Balance Right Away

Once you start becoming aware of your energy, you will know immediately when something has happened that puts you out of balance and you are ready to release the energy.

For example, maybe you get frustrated with a car while you are driving, or something happens at work, or with a family member. Since you are becoming more aware of your energy, you will notice immediately when you feel out of balance, because of an added tension, stress, or negativity into your body. You will not like it (and this is good). You will realize that you do not need a big letting go process to get rid of this, just something simple and easy. Here are some things you can do, but feel free to come up with your own (listen to what your body would like to do to get rid of this energy):

Take deep breaths:

Breathe in White Light, release any negativity, stress, or tension you are feeling when you exhale. Do this three times or until you feel balance.

Draw or paint:

Just remember you are going to recycle or put in the trash when you are done. If you hold onto your creation, you will be holding onto some of the energy you were trying to release.

Talk to someone:

Imagine you are watching your story through their eyes. Look at your situation objectively. Release as you are talking to them, (do not give them this energy; send it up into the Universe or sky.)

Meditate:

Sometimes in meditation, you will find yourself releasing old beliefs and fears.

Go for a walk or hike:

With each step, imagine you are stomping the negativity into the ground. As the negativity hits the ground, it disappears.

"Conscious" exercise:

As you do your daily workout routine, use this time to also release any frustrations, stress, and tension from your day. As you step on the treadmill, push the energy out of your feet. As you lift a weight, punch the energy into the sky.

Stretch:

As you stretch, push out any kinks, stress, and tension in your body and fill that space with White Light.

Spend time in nature:

You can crinkle old leaves in your hand or break sticks. You can throw rocks.

Delete old email:

Deleting junk email or any emails that have hurt you are great ways to release negativity. Deleting old contacts in your address book or phone is also very therapeutic and cleansing.

Walk on the beach:

You can sit in the sand at a beach and give your energy to the waves of water. You can stomp the negativity into the sand. (Remember, the waves are a part of the Universe which is only love. Any negativity will disappear instantly and turn into love.)

Watch a candle burn:

You can give your stress to the candle flame. Often it will give off black smoke and when you are done, it will go back to normal.

Take a shower:

As the water hits your head, imagine it cleansing your body of this energy. Any negativity goes down the drain.

These are some ways to quickly get back in balance. What will help you get back in balance in this moment?

When is My Session Done?

Each person has their own process and timing for letting go of different beliefs in their body. To try and focus on everything all at once is overwhelming to your body and mind.

Do as much at one time as you feel comfortable with in one sitting, but be aware of how your body is feeling. You will know when you are done. You will feel finished and complete. Your "I am" statement will feel true; it will not be a question. You will know you are.

Letting go is very intense energy work. You will feel great when you are done if you do it in a balanced way for your body. The goal is to feel refreshed and recharged when you are done, not to feel like you ran a marathon. After all, you are human, and your body can only experience so much emotion at a time.

Struggling with Your "I am" Statement

If you feel like you are fighting with a part of yourself and you are not connecting with your "I am" statement, try standing under a light or outside under the sun. You can use your hands to trace where the energy is flowing through your body (without touching your body).

If that does not work, try surrounding that area of your body with pink light, and push the negativity, darkness, smoke (whatever you are seeing), out of your body and into the Universe. Then fill that space with pink light. After a letting go session, sometimes a soft pink light will feel more supportive and nurturing to you in that moment. Keep the soft pink light flowing through that area of your body until you feel like whatever was preventing you from bringing the White Light through your body is gone and you are able to connect with your "I am" statement. You will know the negativity is gone when you are able to fill the space with the pink light easily.

Then fill your whole body with pink light. Bring the White Light through your body, into your feet, and into the Earth.

Use your "I am" statements. "I am love. I am safe. I am whole. My body is filled with love. I am _____."

Supporting Your Body

Once you are done with your letting go session, it is very important to pamper your body. You may decide to take it easy the rest of the day or at least for some time following your session.

Drink plenty of water. As you drink the water, imagine you are cleansing your body, flushing out any residual negativity. Then, when you go to the bathroom, imagine you are eliminating it from your body.

Sometimes your body will crave something comforting. It may

be a special soup, tea, food, chair, blanket, etc. If it feels like something that will support you and pamper your body, then do it.

Appreciating Yourself and Your Process

After you do a letting go session, it is important to acknowledge and appreciate the work you have done and the journey you are on. Celebration is vital. It signifies the end of that era of thinking, doing, or being.

It can be something simple and easy. It can be a special trip to a body of water near your home. It can be a hike. It can be pampering yourself or giving yourself a special food. Whatever feels like a celebration to you is what you should do.

How will you celebrate the letting go you did today?

The Waiting Place

Sometimes you will find yourself in a place where it feels like nothing is happening and you feel very stuck. In the Waiting Place, there is a lot of letting go to be done.

There is a peace that is experienced in nature before a change occurs, often a storm. Metaphorically, this is your quiet time before you create a change in your life. Sometimes you chose this change consciously (deliberately), and sometimes you chose it subconsciously, (you will feel as if this change happens to you.)

Often, you get to the Waiting Place after a ton of stuff has been happening. It will feel like you were going a hundred miles an hour and all of a sudden you came to a screeching halt.

This is a place where everything seems still, like nothing is happening. It feels like winter. Remember, things are happening even if you do not feel it. Sometimes you just need to have some quiet space to help you have energy for the new things you have been creating.

Regardless of how and when you get to The Waiting Place, no matter what you do, you cannot force this process to go faster. It feels like you are stuck in limbo. There are things you can do while you are in this place to prepare you for what is ahead. It helps to know what the process is.

Always start by finding the White Light, no matter how small it may seem (it is always everywhere), and remember that you are not alone. You are on your path and in this period of time you are energetically preparing you for the rest of your journey. "I am _____."

During this time, you are switching between these processes:

* Go, go, go!
* Waiting…
* Ready to go!
* It all worked out perfectly!

You will make it through each phase of this process. Here are some clues to help you know where you are at in the process and to make it easier for you to process:

Go, Go, Go!

When you get to The Waiting Place, the "go, go, go" phase is over. Often, you will not even realize this phase happened until you are in the middle of this whole process. You will know it happened because you were extremely busy and life felt crazy. You will be very tired and often you get sick as this process nears the end.

Waiting...

Typically you are exhausted at this point. Your first reaction here is often to get caught up on your rest and things you have been putting to the side. You start this process off feeling great because you have time to get caught up and after all the craziness of "go, go, go" it is nice to have a break.

You will start to get comfortable with this slower pace. Until one day, enough is enough, you are done waiting. You will move into the next stage.

Ready to Go!

I am ready to GO! I have been waiting for so long, why is nothing happening? Why is this taking so long?

This is when the impatience starts. You feel that you are all caught up, that you are ready to go, yet it feels like nothing is happening. This is the phase that people get the most frustrated in because they want to do something, but nothing appears to be happening. Remember, just because you do not see something happening does not mean it is not happening. Trust is key here. The Universe provides us things we cannot see coming and do not understand all the time. This time is no different. Letting go is very helpful here.

You can let go of:
- Your frustration with this process
- Any fears that are coming up for you
- Any irritation from the go, go, go process
- Anything that is keeping you from staying positive and balanced

Trust that: Everything works out perfectly in the best way possible for everyone involved.

Raft Exercise

At this point, it is very helpful to have some idea of where you are at and what you are experiencing. You can do this by imagining that you are on a raft. It can be in the ocean, in a lake, or in a stream.

1 - Close your eyes and imagine yourself on the raft. Whatever type of water you see, that is where you are to be.

2 - How am I reacting on the raft? Notice:
- Am I panicking and clinging on for dear life?
- Am I going with the flow?
- Am I at peace?
- Am I on the raft?
- Am I struggling to stay afloat far away from it?
- What is around me?
- Is the water smooth or rough?

- Are there rocks around me?
- Is there a storm, a rainbow, sun, or clouds in the sky?

3 - What can I do to feel calm, connected to the Universe, and balanced?

Where is the White Light? Bring it through your body, onto the raft, and into the water.

4 - What images from this can I take with me to help support me today?

The water and environment will reflect what is going on. What is important to be aware of here is not what is going on around you, but how you react to what is going on around you.

If you are calm, even if you are heading towards a rocky course, you will feel better as you go through this. You will find things throughout the day that make you happy and you will feel like you are in a better place, because you are.

However, if you are holding on to the raft with clenched fists or if you are panicking in any way, you will find that each day seems hard. Instead of looking for things to help you get through this, you will be noticing things that show you how stuck you are.

If you find yourself here, go back to the raft and relax. Bring the White Light through your body; imagine yourself surrounded by the colors of the rainbow. Once you are feeling calm and balanced, check in with yourself and see what letting go you can do.

Check in with yourself through this raft exercise at least once a day while you are in The Waiting Place. Sometimes it is helpful to do it in the morning and in the evening. Use this as a tool to help you see how you are doing and help you find any areas that could use a little tweak.

It All Worked Out Perfectly!

This phase is celebratory as you will notice, "It all worked out perfectly," once you are through this whole experience.

You will feel at peace momentarily before you move on to whatever is next. After all, if you did not move on to something else, you would still be in a phase of this experience's process.

Notice the moment you feel this peace and create closure.

Typically people move on from one thing to the next, but since you are paying attention to your energy and making sure you are balanced, it is important to give this experience closure by celebrating and appreciating it. Do something to appreciate this experience and everything that you learned. What can you do to celebrate completing this process? This whole process is not something people go through often, but if you do the tips in this section, it will get easier each time.

Releasing an Energy

Being that everything is energy, sometimes you may allow an energy into your energy system to "help" you. I use quotations marks because the energy does not really help you, it uses you, but it wants you to think you need it and it is helping you so it can stay. The energy is something that has to be let go of, but it is a little different than a typical letting go session.

This energy could be a spirit, it could be an energy that has tapped into your chakras (energy system in your body), or perhaps it is an energy that you let someone else give to you subconsciously, as in a curse. The energy can be attached to you or to a space where you live or work.

Typically, you will notice that something is not right. Maybe a room that is clean feels dirty or your hands will feel dirty when they are not. Perhaps you will hear something in your ear or see something go by and there is nothing around you. These are a few ways to become aware of something being attached to you or around you. Once you know it is there, you will agree; it is time to let it go.

Spirits

Spirits are different from other energies in the respect that spirits are love, they are light like us. They are us without a physical body on this plane (where we are currently living). A spirit will not tap into your energy or plug into you. Rather, it gets energy by simply being near you.

How spirits get trapped on this plane:

Perhaps they stay because their family is begging them not to cross over as they are passing and they ignore the White Light that they should cross over in. After some time, they do not see the White Light to cross over into, and they feel stuck or trapped on this plane.

Sometimes they think that if they cross over, they will not be able to tie up loose ends (which they can do easily if they cross over). This can happen if someone dies suddenly, if they have small children, or unfinished business.

Spirits that were addicted to alcohol or drugs like to hang around people and places where these activities are done (you can sense this in bars). Sometimes their addiction is so strong, that even when the body is no longer here, they stay to be near others who share their addiction. By being near them, they can sense their addiction and they often are not interested in crossing over.

Sensing a Spirit

Just because you see a spirit does not mean you have to do something with the spirit. If it is not in your house or bothering you in any way, you can just let it be.

Often, they prefer to be left alone unless you have a spirit that would like to cross over. Spirits can communicate with you in many different ways:

* They can speak to you and you will hear them as if you are talking to yourself, or maybe you can hear them with your ears.
* Sometimes you can sense them and know how you can help.
* They can also be seen with your eyes. Whether you see

colors, sense something flitting by you, or you can see them in some variation of the human form they had.

Releasing a Spirit

If they are in your house or somewhere they should not be, you can ask them nicely to leave. They cannot stay in your space with your energy without your permission, consciously or subconsciously. If you are out in nature and they would like to stay, let them be.

If they do not want to go and they are in your house, ask them why they are there and how you can help them leave. Often they are trapped, they would like to leave but they do not know how to cross over. At this point, you will give them the White Light (see below).

If they are attached to an object (this would be an object that was not new when you acquired it), you can also get rid of that object and they will follow that if you are willing to part with that object.

You can always offer a spirit White Light to help them cross over. They may or may not take it.

Offering a Spirit White Light Exercise

1 - Bring the White Light through your crown, through your body, into your feet, and into the Earth.

2 - Imagine a beam of White Light coming from the sky (like the

beams of light that you see breaking through clouds), to the spirit. (Note: you will keep yourself in White Light through this whole experience; you give them their own White Light.)

Tell the spirit that it is okay for them to go into the light. Depending on how you are sensing the spirit determines how you communicate with it. Only do what you are comfortable with.

If they are interested in going to the light, they will go. If not, that is okay too. They will cross over when they are ready. You may see or feel them cross over. Sometimes you may just sense that they are gone.

If the spirit is in your house and they do not go into the White Light, tell them it is okay if they do not go now into the light, but they can no longer stay here. This will either get them to leave or they will go to the White Light.

3 - Bring the White Light back through your body from your crown, into your feet, and into the Earth.

Other Energies

Sometimes these energies are called entities, negative energy, or demons. Regardless of what you call them, they are simply the absence of love. They use you to tap into your Chakras and have energy. Therefore, they are not real unless we give them power or energy. Since we are made of energy, we provide a place for the energy to literally plug in and thrive.

They begin the size of a speck of pepper and they can grow as tall as the Empire State Building if we let them. These energies are fear based, negative, and pretend to help. At night, it is easier to see them and talk to them, although it may seem scary in the dark as they have more illusion of power at this time. It is easier to see light in the light and dark in the dark.

For a specific reason in this life experience or in another life experience you let this energy attach to you. Perhaps you were a child playing a scary game or as an adult you were afraid and took this negative energy on to "help" you through something. The energy was able to attach to you in a moment when you were scared or afraid of something and the energy seemed safer than the alternative in that moment. Basically, the energy appealed to you and you allowed it to "help" you by attaching into your energy. However, the energy takes more energy from you and keeps you stuck and fearing whatever you allowed it to "help" you with at the time. Now that things are happening to make you aware of it, it is time to let it go. Once you are aware of an energy that is your sign that you no longer "need" its help. You are ready to let it go and fill that space with something that will support you, an "I am safe" statement, or whatever "I am" you feel will support you the most in this moment.

It may seem scary since it will talk back to you, but when it talks, it is telling you how you let it in to "help" you. The energy will give you the clues to let it go. Objectively listen to what it says. If it is telling you that it makes you safe, it protects you from getting hurt, or anything like that, start there!

White Light conquers all, so it will make this energy disappear back to a speck of pepper and vanish into White Light.

Sometimes it does not matter what it is. Sometimes it is important to know what it is, why it is here, and how it was "helping" you. You will know if this is important as you are doing your letting go.

Letting go of an energy is very similar to a visual letting go (see Visualizing Exercise). The only thing that is different is that you are getting rid of a specific energy that is attached to your body that you are finished with as it is no longer "helping" you.

Sometimes when you release this energy, you will become aware of another energy or two that is also ready to be released. It is very easy to release other energies in a session once you release the first one.

Do not be afraid when you see these energies. Remember, they are simply the absence of love. Anything not of love is not real unless you give it power. You are not giving it power, you are letting it go. Surround yourself with as much light as possible if that helps you remember that you are light. Light always conquers the darkness. Think about a dark room and what happens when you turn on a light, the darkness disappears. It is no longer real. This is the same. Once you turn on the White Light, the darkness will disappear.

Releasing an Energy Exercise

1 - Bring the White Light through your crown (top of your head), through your body, into your feet, and into the Earth. "I am love, I am light, I am safe, I am whole."

Note: The energy may be laughing or telling you that you are not one or several of these things. Use this to help fuel you in letting it go. Of course you are love, light, and safe. Because it is telling you that you are not, is proof that it is not "helping" you, and that it is time to let it go.

2 - Notice where you are able to sense the energy in your body. Start with the area that is calling your attention the most. Often the energy starts in one place and has roots like a plant going to another part of your body. The energy tries to anchor to you in such a way that it may seem difficult to sense where it begins and where it ends. Instead of trying to figure it out, close your eyes and ask yourself, "where should I start?" Start there.

3 - Imagine that you are pulling this energy out like a weed. Sometimes it seems deep, but just keep pulling it out or releasing it like smoke (or whatever visual comes to you). Whatever you see and feels right to you in that moment, do. Imagine sending that energy up into the sky or the Universe. Remember, the Universe is love and only love. The Universe will turn the energy into love and it will disappear. This will not hurt the Universe in any way.

4 - What is the energy saying to you? How is it trying to persuade you to keep it? At this point, it will be stating its purpose, its cause, why you "need" it, and have to have it. Remember, the energy is using you; you do not have to use it and you do not "need" it in any way. The energy does not really help you, it just pretends to. This energy is an illusion; it is the absence of love. Let it go.

Why did you allow it to attach to you?

How is this energy "helping" you?

Thank the energy for its "help". The energy has quite the ego and likes to be appreciated for its work. Thank it simply. For example: Thank you for "helping" me feel safe.

Feel free to have a conversation with this energy in your head or out loud if you feel comfortable. Bring in the White Light and use your "I am" statements as often as you would like through this process.

5- "I am love, I am light, I am safe," perhaps add in "I am whole," and whatever other "I am" statement that supports you in releasing this specific energy.

Sometimes it helps to wiggle or shake that body part.

6- When it feels like it is gone, bring the White Light through your body again. "I am _____."

7- After you have brought the White Light through your body, check in with yourself. Does it feel gone? No? Keep going for as long as you can. Remember to stay in balance with your body. If you are feeling that your body has done all it can right now then do more another day. Sometimes it takes a few times to release an energy if it is really rooted in your system.

When the energy is gone, ask yourself if there is another energy to let go of somewhere else in body? If you answer yes, release that energy if you can at this moment.

8 - Check in again and see if there is anything else to let go of in this moment.

When you feel done and complete (even if it is just for now), bring the White Light through your body. "I am _____."

For a Few Days After Releasing an Energy:
* Say your "I am" statements.
* Drink plenty of water and imagine you are flushing any remnants out of your body.
* Bring the White Light through your body several times a day.

You may notice that in the dark or at night, you can sense the energy again. Chances are it is not attached to you, but reappearing to make sure you really meant for it to leave.

This happens because you took the energy on in a moment of weakness (you were feeling vulnerable about something), and it is hoping to catch you again, as if you made a mistake and you desperately need that energy again.

If the energy comes back, simply say, "no thank you," or "go away." Put yourself in White Light. Then say your "I am" statements that helped you release the energy. "I am love. I am safe. I am whole. I am _____." You can also fill your body with a soft pink light.

The energy typically comes back once or a few times over three days. Stay strong. You are love and do not require any darkness in your being. The energy knows that, but it needs you. Without your energy, it cannot exist. Do not let it in and it will go away.

Releasing a Curse

A curse is simply allowing someone else to give you some form of negative energy or darkness. For whatever reason, you allow this energy in subconsciously, meaning you have taken on this energy without realizing what you were doing.

If you can sense it, it will feel heavy and you may feel dirty, like there is something sticking to your body and you want to wash it off but it will not come off. Also, you will not be able to bring the White Light down through your crown and through your body, this is a big sign that this has happened. Typically you will know this energy is here because someone who can read this type of energy can see it on you. Usually most people are not aware of this energy being on them.

A curse is different than "other energies" in that it feels heavy, like a cloak, hanging over your whole body. Curses affect your whole body, not just one part of it. It is as if this cloak is trying to smother you in darkness so you forget about the White Light, but the White Light is always there.

Since this energy is not light, and it is not love, it is something to be released. You will surround yourself in White Light and use "I am" statements in this release. What is different in this releasing is that you will start at your feet and work your way up to your head since this energy is blocking your head from the light. This will only take a few minutes. Energy moves quickly.

Releasing a Curse Exercise

1 - Sit comfortably and do not cross your legs. It may be helpful for you to sit in the sun or under a light to help you see the light.

2 - Imagine the White Light at your feet. As you move the White Light up your body it will push the darkness out of your body.

Imagine the White Light spreading from the Earth, to your feet, up your legs to your knees, then to your thighs, to your hips, your stomach, your chest and back, your neck, your head, and up through your crown.

Imagine the White Light pushing the darkness away and up into the Universe.

3 - Then bring the White Light through your body again from your crown, through your body, into your feet, and into the Earth.

Say: "I am love. I am safe. I am whole."

4 - Imagine a pink swirl going around the outside of your body, starting above your head and going into the Earth.

For a few days after releasing a curse:

* Say your "I am" statements.

* Drink plenty of water and imagine you are flushing any remnants out of your body.
* Bring the White Light through your body several times a day.

Overview

Experiment with different ways of letting go. Learn what works best for you to get back into balance. Different situations require different approaches.

Notice where you hold tension in your body. As you feel yourself absorbing this energy in a situation, stop! Realize what you are doing and instead of absorbing that energy, do not allow it in. Do not build a wall, but do not take it in.

ALWAYS discard any letting go creations (for example, artwork, journaling, etc.), by burning or throwing in the trash when completed to provide closure. Make sure you put it in its final resting place before you end your letting go session. Somewhere you will not think about it again. Otherwise, you will have to move it again and add more closure.

Be objective when letting go. There is no good or bad. There is no label unless you give it one. Everything is as it should be. Look at things objectively and release your attachment to them so you can let things go more easily.

Letting go does not have to take a long time. Energy moves quickly. You will know when you are done. Most sessions can be done in five to fifteen minutes total.

Soft pink, soft blue, soft green, or soft purple light can feel very nurturing after any letting go session. You can bring one or many of these colors through your body any time after White Light. Just imagine that color going through your body just like the White Light does. You may also feel supported by wearing those colors, putting those color stones in your pocket, or even writing your "I am" statements on paper that is that color.

5 - Living in Balance with Others

Now that you are more aware of your energy, it is time to become aware of how you are using your energy with other people.

You are surrounded by people when you are on the freeway, in line at a store, and when you go for a walk at the park. These people influence you just as much as the people that live in your house or that work with you. It is important to become aware of your energy in all of these interactions so you stay balanced.

Becoming Energy Conscious

As you start to become aware of your energy, you will become more sensitive to the energy around you. You may notice that you are picking up on the energy of the people or the environment around you.

For example:

* When you stand next to someone who is angry, you may feel a sudden headache that goes away when one of you walks away or when you pull out of their energy (you notice the headache is not yours and you stop allowing that energy into your body.)
* Someone may be telling you a story and you feel tension in your legs, hips, stomach, or chest. You can pull out of their

energy whenever you want. Just imagine pulling your energy back to you and focus on your body. You can bring the White Light through your body to help change your focus as well as help you rebalance your body.

* You may feel like you do not want to walk into a building or go to a certain place.
* You may know what someone is thinking or what energy they are giving off to others around them.

You will respond differently in different situations. Pay attention to when you are noticing a shift in your body. If you do not want to pick up on someone else's energy at the moment, do not. You always have a choice. However, if you are supposed to do something to help someone and you keep ignoring it, the energy you are noticing will get more and more intense until you help the other person (see Helping Others on the next page.)

Become aware of your energy throughout the day:

* Check in with yourself and notice where you are putting your energy (your frustration, fears, self-doubts).
* Is any part of your body tense?
* Are you putting up walls?
* Are you taking on other people's "stuff"? Should you be?

Staying in balance means that you are aware of what you are doing with your energy in any given moment. The moment you notice yourself getting out of balance, ask yourself what you can do to get back in balance. Perhaps a mini meditation, a mini letting go session, or some time relaxing will help you.

Helping Others

Now that you are aware of your energy and other people's energy, what do you do with all of this and how do you stay in balance?

When you are in balance, you can easily see where other people may not be. Your instinct may be to jump in and help them.

When not to Help Someone

You can only help others when they would like to be helped. This is a big concept. How can someone not be interested in changing and feeling better? Especially when you can see so clearly what would help them at this moment, and they are not interested.

Simply stated, we are where we are. If someone is not interested in changing, you cannot make them. You will find if you are helping someone who does not ask for your help, it actually makes things complicated for both of you. Sometimes they will get mad at you for trying to help when they did not ask for it.

You cannot make the alcoholic stop drinking, or the drug abuser stop using. You can put them into rehabilitation multiple times, but until someone has decided to make a change in their life, you cannot make them change without their willingness to work with you. Even if it is something simple like being aware of the words they are using, if they are not interested in changing, there is nothing you can do to make them change.

What you can do is be there for them when they are ready. Until then:

* You can send them White Light. You can give it to people, but they have to accept it at some level. (See Sharing White Light with Others, page 112.)
* You can surrender the situation to the White Light. (See Surrendering a Situation to White Light, page 113.)
* You can just let them be. This may be difficult for you to do, but remember, you can only help people that would like help. Otherwise you are causing a lot of unnecessary pain for both of you.

If people are interested in being dysfunctional and you are trying to get them to be another way, they do not see that as helpful. Instead, it makes them feel like they have to work harder at being dysfunctional.

When to Help Someone

If people are interested in your help, they will be eager for feedback and tips on ways to get back on track. If you start to feel that helping them is too much, be honest with them. Once you start attracting people to you that are interested in receiving your help, you will find you are not interested in trying to help someone that does not want your help in the first place. When you are helping someone:

* Do not judge or try to understand how you are getting to help them. Perhaps you say something to them that makes complete sense to them, but you have no idea what it means.

* Maybe you can feel where they are holding onto energy in their body. For me the throbbing, pain, numbness (whatever the physical feeling is), gets stronger until I explain it in such a way that the person is able to connect with it. As soon as they connect with it, they take on the work, it lessens in my body, and goes away completely once I have helped them let it go.

Make sure your ego is not involved. It is not important for you to be right and for them to be wrong. Instead, share your sense, feeling, or intuition with them and then let it go. Do not hold onto any of their stuff, even if it is to see if you were right with what you were getting to share. Things are constantly shifting and changing. Whatever you are sharing with them in the moment is true for them, and then move on, let it go.

The more you help others, the more practice you will get. Remember, by taking on their stuff, it does not help you or them. Their stuff just doubles, meaning you take it on for them and they take it back on too, since they were not done with it. Then you both have it. Always let people get rid of their own "stuff". You can just be there as a support that does not take it on.

Feel Safe without Building Walls

Walls are often built to help you feel safe and protected. Building walls and even forts around you to "protect" you takes a lot of energy. If you have been building walls, forts, or even castles to help you feel safe, ask yourself, "Do I feel safe?"

The response I get from clients is no. The walls do not help you feel safe, which is how they turn into forts, or castles with moats. The walls you build keep getting bigger and bigger and as you can imagine, this takes quite a bit of energy, yet you still do not feel safe. Instead:

* Bring the White Light through you and then let it go where it would like to.
* Imagine surrounding yourself in a soft blanket of whatever pastel color pops into your mind. Typically it will start off as a pink blanket and over time it will become different colors depending on what is going on around you.
* Let the walls (or castles and forts), fall down and disappear.
* Say: "I am safe. I am love. I am whole," and believe it. If you are not able to believe it, then there is some letting go to do. Then say these "I am" statements again.
* Know that you are always love and you are always safe. The White Light is within you and you can be near or even surrounded in darkness and not have it affect you because you are in White Light.

White Light makes the darkness disappear. The darkness is an illusion and you are filled with love. Love always conquers all, therefore you are always safe. Remember, whenever you turn a light on in a dark room, the darkness goes away. The same thing applies here.

Changing Your Dance with Others

As you start to become aware of your energy, you will notice the dances you have been doing with others.

Dances are energy exchanges where someone uses their power to get you to do something and you do it.

Whether they are your parents, your siblings, your significant other, work colleagues, or friends, as you change, they try to get you back to how you used to be. It is not that they are interested in keeping you stuck in this pattern and dance, it is all they know. This is the way you have been interacting with them and perhaps they do not know another way, or they are not comfortable with another way, since this is something they have been doing for a very long time.

Once you start to feel balance, the last thing you are interested in doing is anything you know that intentionally puts you back out of balance. Often, these dances put you out of balance very quickly.

When someone starts to do a dance with you that you are no longer interested in doing, simply give the energy back to them. Instead of accepting the energy and allowing it into your body, imagine that you are pushing it away with your hands or say, "no thank you" with your mind.

The Dance

They do "this" and you do "that". No matter what happens, every time they do "this" you do "that".

If you try to change this dance, they keep doing "this" in many different ways and it seems they are throwing all kinds of energy at you in different angles to get the typical "that" back from you, until eventually they do.

For example:

A family member calls you up complaining about another family member and they just cannot stand what they are doing. They want (here is that "want" word), you to stop whatever you are doing and get involved and fix it. Normally you would, for whatever reason, it is always so compelling and you always get involved, so you just stop whatever you are doing and do it.

But now that you are aware of your energy and what this person is doing, you are not interested in doing your typical dance with them.

This will completely throw off the other person for a minute but they will rebound quickly, trying to find other ways to get you involved and into their cause.

At this point, your job is to not do your typical dance, no matter what they say or do. Really, it is not your business and it will just cause you problems with this third person, and throw you out of balance.

Bring the White Light in and imagine all the energy they keep throwing at you (trying to get you to do this typical dance), just bounces right off of you and goes back to them. It does not hurt them, it is their energy. You are simply not accepting this energy and you are giving it back.

They will keep trying many different persuasive ways to get you to do this dance. After all, it is what you have always done together.

Eventually they will stop trying the dance with you. You may notice them looking at you differently or they may even laugh. They are not sure what just happened. They will try again, in other ways to change the dance so they can get their desired outcome from you.

Just know that when they do, you changed the dance once and you will be able to change it again.

Being Aware of Your Energy in a Conflict

Next time you are in a personal situation that is emotionally charged, pay attention to your energy and notice how differently the situation can be resolved when you are being energy conscious.

Start by imagining you are watching the situation on TV or in a movie and you have no emotional ties to what is happening, even though it is directly affecting you and happening to you. This is very important! Be objective no matter what they say or do. Notice what the other person is really saying to you. Pay attention to the words they are using and their nonverbal actions.

* What is it that they would like to change?
* How does this change affect you?
* Are you able or willing to make this change? If not, what is a good compromise or middle ground?

Breathe before you respond. (This will give you time to think about what you are going to say too.) Focus on the breath you are taking and it cleansing your body, pushing out any irritation or frustration as you exhale.

Think about what you would like to do instead of just responding.

* Is this something to talk about now? Are you able to talk about this objectively? If yes, keep breathing and being objective during the discussion.
* If not, can it wait until later? (Usually the answer here is yes. Do not let your emotions or anger control this conversation or it will be an argument without a purpose with much apologizing later on everyone's part.)

If they do not want to wait until later but it has the potential to end up in a big fight, it is in both of your interests to wait. It is important to frame it in a way so they know you are not putting it off, but that it is probably best for you to both think about this before you talk about it and say things that you cannot take back. Let them know your intention is to create a calm place to have a discussion and create change. After all, that is the purpose of this. Perhaps you can both sit down and write down the key facts that you would like to calmly discuss the next day.

If one person is calm and rational in an emotionally charged situation, it will prevent the whole situation from escalating out of control. There is no point in having a discussion when no one remembers what the original discussion was supposed to be about because it turned into a big fight where both people get hurt.

If you decide to wait until later to talk about it, or you find that neither side is budging, nor any compromise is happening, use this time instead to let go of any frustration and anger.

Look at the Letting Go section of this book and find something that works for you in this moment. Find a safe place to let go of these emotions that are throwing you out of balance.

If you go to bed before you talk about it, it is okay as long as you are in a place of peace with your emotional charge in this situation. When you wake up in the morning, you will feel that you are able to talk about this situation, but you will feel more objective. This only works if you have done the letting go first and you are in as good of a place as you can be before you talk about it with the other person again.

When you do talk about this situation, make sure you are saying things that are true to this situation and not from years ago or even weeks ago. Talking about things from other disagreements that have not been resolved, are not going to get resolved in this space, they will just add more fuel to the fire. All of which leads to an argument where everyone walks away feeling even more unsettled and frustrated.

State your case by using, "I feel _____ when this happens." Be open to finding a solution that works for both or all parties involved.

Once you have reached a solution, what can everyone do to make this a reality? How can everyone check in to make sure that they are doing what they said they would do?

If you were feeling any unresolved anger, frustration, or issues from past disagreements, what can you do to let them go and move forward?

Creating Peace in Relationships from Long Ago

Sometimes you will find that there is a relationship in your past, whether it is in this life or in another life experience that you would like to create peace, and it is not possible for you to physically talk to this person.

Perhaps they have passed (died), or they are someone from your childhood or high school that you lost contact with years ago, and you have been thinking about them or having dreams about them. Maybe they are someone you could physically talk to, but you are not in a place where you feel comfortable doing that yet, but you would like to start bringing peace to this relationship. Regardless of the situation, you are still able to create peace in this relationship.

Creating Peace in a Relationship Exercise

When you are feeling a pull to resolve a relationship from the past, the other person is as well, which is why you are interested in creating peace.

1 - Always begin by creating a safe place. Be somewhere you feel safe and supported physically.

Close your eyes. Bring the White Light through your body starting with your crown and allow the White Light to flow through your whole body, into your feet, and into the Earth.

2 - Relax your mind and imagine the person (deceased or alive), that you would like to speak to. Imagine their face or imagine the situation you would like to heal with peace.

3 - Talk to the person either in your mind or out loud. Whatever you feel comfortable with, either way, they can hear you and they will respond.

Say what you would like to say to them.

Pause.

What do you hear back? Whatever thoughts, images, or words that are coming to you are coming to you from that person. The mind is not able to make this stuff up.

Have a conversation with this person. Allow the situation to be resolved; you are not fighting with this person in any way. Perhaps you are apologizing or you are allowing them to explain why something happened. You can also use this meditation to speak with people that have passed that you would like to share something with, just share your news and wait for them to respond.

4 - When the situation feels complete, you can close it however seems fit and healing to you. Perhaps you say, "thank you," or "I am at peace with this situation."

5 - Bring the White Light into the situation and surround both of you in the White Light.

Bring the White Light through your body from your crown, through your body, into your feet, and into the Earth.

"I am peace. I am whole. We are one. I am _____."

Open your eyes when you are ready.

6 - Living in Balance From Within

Your body gives you signs to help you know when you are in balance and when you are on track.

Paying attention to these signs is important because even when you choose to ignore them, the body will not let you. Little things will get worse.

For example, you cannot ignore a cold that turns into a sinus infection or a cough that turns into bronchitis. Use your body as a guide, pay attention to the signs it gives you. Often, your body may be telling you to slow down. Check in with yourself and ask, "What am I supposed to be doing?" Then do it.

Your body will also tell you if you are not making the best choice for you at this moment. If you feel uneasiness in your stomach after making a decision, take a step back. Consider what other choices or actions you can take and how your body feels as you imagine those other scenarios. What course of action makes you feel the most balanced?

Notice when you feel a headache, tension, or tightness in your body. Ask yourself, "When did I first feel this in my body?" What fears, concerns, or stress are you holding in your body? Then find a way to release the tension, perhaps through deep breathing, walking, swimming, talking, or journaling.

Check in with yourself and see what your body would like or is missing. It may be as simple as taking a walk or eating something your body is craving. Some days it may require some support from a friend, family, or coach.

Be Aware of Your Energy Level

Pay attention to your energy. If your energy is too high or too low, either extreme takes a lot of energy. Our bodies do best when we are not riding energetic rollercoasters.

Some energy fluctuation in the day is normal, but you have to become conscious of where you are putting your energy.

Your Energy is too Low

Notice if your energy is taking a dip. Again, this is okay for a small amount of time, but for too long (this amount of time depends on you), and it will start to really affect you.

Ask yourself why you are feeling low energy and getting stuck here?

Are you tired, upset, angry, and/or depleted from over doing something? If so, let it go.

It is okay to be low energy, but for small periods of time. Do something to bring your energy back up. Breathe (even if only for two minutes), read something inspiring, talk to a friend, use an "I am" statement, or be grateful for something in the moment, basically do something to get back on track.

Your Energy is too High

Also notice if your energy is so high that it feels like you are soaring in the sky like a bird or a kite.

Clues you are not grounded or your energy level is too high for you:

- * You feel like you are floating in the air.
- * You are having a hard time committing to a decision that typically would be easy for you.
- * You are not interested in doing something that will bring you back into the present moment.

This is a more positive experience, a natural high, but if you look at the things happening to your body you will see that it can be very exhausting for your body. Plus, it is very difficult to take action in this place. Everything seems great and fabulous, even when it is not.

You will end up feeling out of balance and most likely you will find that you are not grounded (the White Light is not going through your legs, into your feet, and into the Earth.)

Exercise to Help Ground You:

If you are not balanced or not grounded, begin by sitting down (make sure your legs or arms are not crossed), and slowly bring the White Light through your body.

Imagine the White Light at your crown, going down your head, your neck, your shoulders, your chest and back, to your stomach, your pelvic bones, to your thighs, your knees, your legs to your feet, and down into the Earth.

Focus on feeling the peace and calm of the White Light flowing through your body and into the Earth. You feel grounded, safe, and whole.

Quietly say: "I am safe. I am whole. I am connected with the Earth."

Always check in and make sure you are feeling balanced. If you are on too much of a high or low for a long period of time, your body's natural response is to crash, that means, you will possibly get sick with a virus or something will happen that will cause you to be in bed for a day or two. Once you are down, literally, your body has a chance to get back into balance.

Remember, being too high or too low is hard on the body energetically. Being too high or too low prevents you from "seeing" things clearly. You will have highs and lows, but it is important to pay attention to why you are experiencing something and notice when you have been in one energy state for too long for you.

Balance is very important; you will find that once you are in balance often, you will not like the feeling of being unbalanced.

Learning to Find Your Balance

Now that we have talked about being low energy and high energy, it is time to talk about finding your balanced energy level. This is a place where you are happy, content, and at peace.

In your balanced energy level, life is flowing naturally, everything feels as though it is in its perfect place (even if everything around you is not), and you are relaxed.

Your balance can be experienced in every situation.

To find your balance, just close your eyes and relax. Bring the White Light through your body, into your feet, and into the Earth. You can also close your eyes and imagine yourself doing something that is relaxing to you.

Some examples to imagine are:
* Walking on the beach in the sand
* Relaxing in the bathtub or a hot tub
* Watching the stars
* Sitting in your favorite vacation spot
* Relaxing by a fire

Notice how you feel while you are there. Calm, relaxed, perfectly energized, at complete peace. You are balanced in this state. This is your natural energy level and the energy to recreate for yourself when you are feeling stressed out, tense, overly stimulated, or as though the sky is falling.

Balance is all you knew before any beliefs and ideals were set for you in every situation. You hold the key to your beliefs about your energy and how you are going to use and experience your energy in every situation.

Remember, the goal is to find balance and try to stay as close to balance no matter what is going on around you. There will be fluctuation, after all, that is why we are here having all of these fabulous experiences. The more time you spend being in balance, the more balanced you will feel, the more energy you will have, and you will know how to get back into your balanced state more easily.

Try to keep your energy balanced throughout the day. Notice how your body gets exhausted from a lot of fluctuation (meaning from being low energy, to high, to low, to medium energy). That is exhausting! It is similar to doing a triathlon, going to work, coming home to your family, and then working out again, all in ONE day. You would not physically put your body through that in one day, so be aware of what you are doing to your body energetically. You will find that you will have more energy when you stay in a balanced state.

Balance is key and it is possible to find your balance throughout the day no matter what is going on around you.

Regaining Balance

Everything you are reading in this book is in here to help you find balance. At this point, it should be getting easier for you to tell when you are not in balance.

While you are doing the White Light and "I am" statements, you are in balance. You feel calm, at peace.

Of course, life happens and you get into your routine, which sometimes pushes you way out of balance. Clues you are not in balance:

- * Things are not working out, especially when you have an overbooked schedule.
- * Your body is giving you some physical signs to tell you to get back on track.
- * You feel overwhelmed or stressed out.
- * You keep getting colds and minor ailments.
- * Little things are setting you off and making you seem like a time bomb ready to explode.

Of course, there are many ways your body will tell you that you are not in balance. The more time you spend getting back into balance, the easier it will be to catch yourself getting out of balance.

Life is literally a balancing act. Remember, everything in moderation. Too much of something is not usually a good thing, especially if you are not in balance to begin with.

Exercise to Get Balanced:

Take your time and slowly do this exercise, especially if you are not grounded.

Begin by sitting down (make sure your legs or arms are not crossed), and slowly bring the White Light through your body.

Imagine the White Light at your crown, going down your head, your neck, your shoulders, your chest and back, to your stomach, your pelvic bones, to your thighs, your knees, your legs to your feet, and down into the Earth.

Focus on feeling the peace and calm of the White Light flowing through your body and into the Earth. You feel grounded, safe, and whole.

Quietly say: "I am safe. I am whole. I am connected with the Earth."

As you go about your day, pay special attention to your energy. If you start to feel unbalanced again, quickly think about something you are grateful for and bring the White Light through your body again.

Balance is something we are all working on in this experience. The scales are constantly moving in opposite directions, but you can find your balance in any situation. When you are in balance, you are a well-oiled machine.

As you practice different tips and tools in this book, you will find that it becomes easier to stay in balance. As soon as you get out of balance, notice that you are automatically doing something to help you find it again.

Meditation

Meditation is a way for you to connect with your spirit and find balance. This is a time for you to relax and replenish.

Everyone has time for meditation. You can set a timer for five minutes in the morning and five minutes in the evening before or after dinner. If you can do more, that is great! The more you meditate, the better you will feel physically and mentally. Start with at least five minutes twice a day.

Sit comfortably, so you can focus on your meditation, not the discomforts of your body.

Start by bringing the White Light through your body. Imagine it entering your crown (top of your head), going down your face, your neck, to your chest and back, to your stomach, to your hips, to your thighs, to your knees, down your legs, into your feet, and into the Earth.

Take three deeps breaths. When you breathe in, breathe in the White Light. When you exhale, release any tension in your body.

At this point, let your mind go blank.

Use an "I am" statement as a start to your meditation. This can be your focus for your meditation. Then imagine colors, a serene place in nature, a bird, or whatever pops into your mind that relaxes you.

Go with the flow of what you are seeing and experiencing. If you start trying to think about what you are experiencing, move past the words. Do not give them power by thinking about quieting them. Just imagine you are floating away from them or focus on what you are seeing.

The mind does not understand meditating. It does understand categorizing things and it tries to analyze what you are doing:

"why am I here, why am I seeing this image, what should I do with this image?" Then the meditation is long gone and you are in your mind again. Do not allow your mind to have power in your meditation, just move away from its thoughts and return to your "I am" statement.

When you are done, take a few deep breaths.

"I am love. I am safe. I am whole. I am _____."

Open your eyes when you are ready.

There are many books on meditating and even CD's at the library. Some people like to listen to music to help them relax.

I find that if you set a timer whether on your stove, microwave, or phone, it allows you to relax into your meditation. By setting the timer, you can focus on your meditation and not what you have to do when you are finished with your meditation. Sit up if you can. If you lay down, you will probably fall asleep.

Mini Meditations

Mini meditations are very small meditations you can do throughout the day to help you connect with yourself and find balance.

You can give yourself a minute in the parking lot at work, a minute at your desk before an important meeting, a minute at lunch, a minute before you head into traffic, essentially whenever you feel you can use one.

Start by taking a few deep breaths.

Start by bringing the White Light through your body. Imagine it entering your crown (top of your head), going down your face, your neck, to your chest and back, to your stomach, to your hips, to your thighs, to your knees, down your legs, into your feet, and into the Earth.

Let your spirit go where it would like to go. Perhaps to a meadow with a stream, perhaps to a garden, you will know exactly where you would like to go and what you are supposed to see and do in this mini meditation.

When you are done, take a few deep breaths.

"I am love. I am safe. I am whole. I am _____."

Open your eyes when you are ready.

Color Meditations

Color meditations are very nurturing and supportive to your body. These are good to do after a letting go session and they are helpful in letting you know where there is energy to let go. Color meditations are exactly what they sound like. It is a meditation using different colors in different parts of your body. You will see yourself surrounded by whatever color pops into your mind at each part of your body.

Start by taking a few deep breaths.

Start by bringing the White Light through your body. Imagine it entering your crown (top of your head), going down your face, your neck, to your chest and back, to your stomach, to your hips, to your thighs, to your knees, down your legs, into your feet, and into the Earth.

Now it is time to bring in color. Note: Sometimes people like to imagine light touching each part of their body. Sometimes it is helpful to imagine you are surrounding yourself in a soft blanket that is whatever color that part of your body would like. Another option is to imagine moving the energy around each part of your body like a spiral. Do what is most comfortable for you. If you see any black or darkness, that is a sign that you have letting go to do in that area.

Start by bringing a color in to the top of your head (crown) and to your face.

Imagine a different color on: your throat, shoulders, chest and back, stomach, hips, thighs, knees, legs, and your feet. Imagine this color from your feet going into the Earth.

For example:

Start by bringing a soft purple in to the top of your head (crown) and to your face.

Imagine:

A soft green on your throat and shoulders,

A soft pink on your chest and back,

A soft orange color as you go to your stomach,

A soft blue as you go to your hips,

A warm turquoise color as you go to your thighs,

A soft yellow as you go to your knees,

A light green as you go to your legs and

A sparkling gold as you go to your feet. Imagine this color from your feet going into the Earth.

Note: The colors I see in each area are different every time, just as it will be for you. This is just an example to help you see how a color meditation may go. Use the colors that literally pop into your mind as you go through your body. Do not think about it, just see it. If you are aware of what colors go to each chakra, do not put the chakra colors where they typically are, because that may not be the colors that area would like to have. If you are seeing primary colors, this is an area that could use some White Light. It is not a bad thing to see these colors, it is just a way for your body to say, "Hey, look at this area."

Remember, if you see any darkness or smoke, this is energy your body is ready to let go of. You are seeing it so you can let it go. At this point, it may be helpful to do a "Visualize" letting go exercise.

Sometimes you will see sparkling colors or symbols. Whatever you see is what you are supposed to do for your body.

When you are done, take a few deep breaths. "I am love. I am safe. I am whole. I am _____."

Open your eyes when you are ready.

Meditation to Heal the Earth

This meditation is to help heal our world. We live in different continents, but we are all one, therefore we are all connected. We feel what is happening in other parts of the world even if it is not happening in our neighborhood, and it is always helpful to send White Light.

Start by taking a few deep breaths.

Then bring the White Light through your body. Imagine it entering your crown (top of your head), going down your face, your neck, to your chest and back, to your stomach, to your hips, to your thighs, to your knees, down your legs, into your feet, and into the Earth.

Imagine that you approach the Earth and there is a circle of people or angels doing this meditation, standing around it. It is a safe space.

As you enter the circle, send White Light to the person next to you. Typically the energy goes from right to left, but it is possible to start on the left sometimes. They send the White Light to the person next to them and it continues until it is given back to you.

Together, you start at the core of the Earth and you see the White Light radiating out of it like the sun. Slowly, the White Light grows larger and expands until it covers the Earth and it reaches out to the circle. Go slow. If you move too fast, you will find that this does more harm than good. Go at a pace that feels comfortable and right during your meditation.

At this point, let the meditation guide you, go with the flow. Some things you may notice in your meditation:

Animals: Notice what they are doing. Are they afraid, losing their habitat, thirsty or hungry, feeling the effects of the people around them? How can you help them?

Trees, plants, vegetation: Are they frozen? Are they dry? How can you help them in the meditation?

Water: Oceans, lakes, rivers, streams, and the habitats inside of them. What are they experiencing and how can you help?

People: Are they fighting? Are they at peace? Release their negativity. Sometimes on the outer edge of the Earth (where the people live), you will notice the tension and darkness. Help them lift this darkness, send the darkness up into the Universe where it will turn into love and disappear. Surround the people in White Light.

Different hemispheres: Notice the energy in different parts. Are they balanced? Can one part use more White Light and love? Send it to them.

Colors: Sometimes you will see many different colors (like the Color Meditations); sometimes you will see one color throughout the meditation. Occasionally you will notice symbols in silver or gold mixed in with the colors. Let them flow. Do not question them or try to figure out what they are. Let them do their work.

Seasons: The effects of the temperature on the land and its inhabitants: In the winter you may notice the freezing cold and in the summer the scorching heat and lack of water. What would the land like to have? What can you visualize sending it?

Weather: Do you notice a storm? How is it affecting the inhabitants of the area? Do you see cracks in the dry Earth? Do you sense an earthquake? How can you help in the meditation?

Regardless of what you see in your meditation, and you will see many different things each time, offer White Light, love, and peace. Every meditation will be different depending on what is happening with the Earth and its inhabitants. Your job in this meditation is to support the Earth and its inhabitants.

Remember to be aware of your energy throughout the meditation. Notice the impact of the energy you are working with on your body.

* Do your arms or back feel heavy?
* Do you feel tension in your legs?
* Do you feel extremely hot or cold?

These are things to pay attention to and if you notice you are feeling something, simply release it up into the Universe. You can imagine it as smoke, or just see and feel the tension floating away and being surrounded by love.

When the meditation feels complete or your time is done, return back to the original circle around the Earth. Send White Light to the person who gave it to you last. Watch the White Light get passed to each person until it returns back to you.

Check your energy again. Are you carrying any energy from the

Earth in your body? If you are, release it back to the Universe and watch it turn into love or a speck of White Light.

When you are finished with the meditation:

Bring the White Light through your body. Imagine it entering your crown (top of your head), going down your face, your neck, to your chest and back, to your stomach, to your hips, to your thighs, to your knees, down your legs, into your feet, and into the Earth.

Take a few deep breaths.

"I am love. I am safe. I am whole. Love flows through the Universe."

Open your eyes when you are ready.

7 - We Are All One

A Ball of White Light

Before we began our journeys, we were all together in a big ball of White Light. The center is warm and nurturing and it shines throughout the ball, like a sun's rays.

Love, peace, and happiness are our core. It is all we know in the ball. It is our truth. We are all one, we are all connected. We are peace. We are able to easily reconnect with this when we meditate.

We decided to experience what it would feel like to be separate from the ball of White Light. How else would we truly appreciate these things that we know to be true without knowing what the opposite feels like?

In our bodies, we feel separate and disconnected from each other. Our mind helps act as a filter, creating a "me" space instead of a "we" mentality. We think, "I can get mad at you, or hurt you, and it is okay because I think that you are separate from me." We forget that we are connected, and if I get mad at you, or I hurt you, I will feel it immediately since I am doing it to myself as well.

Our truth: we are all one. This means that we are literally all connected to each other. We are not separate even though our bodies appear to be. Some people can see the energy that connects us to each other. Where you would think one energy ends, it just blends into the next. We are all energetically connected to each other and the living things around us, including the Earth.

Karma

What I do to you, I do to myself. This happens because I am you and you are me. Karma happens instantly and often across many different lives. This is a big concept that is very difficult for our mind and ego to understand. We do not have to understand it to believe it, but if you meditate you can sense it all, and it makes sense.

How We Store Our Energy Across Lives

We live all of our lives at one time. There is no chronological timeline of A to Z. Everything happens at once, simultaneously. We energetically store information across our life experiences and we have access to them in every experience. That is how you can be letting go and see that this energy in your knee is from when you were hurt farming and you felt abandoned on the field, or what have you.

Often our past fears keep coming up and they try to take over. We hold onto our experiences, fears, and everything that came with it to remember. Perhaps we think we will not do it again, but because we are holding onto it, we will do it again and again. Fears actually force us to keep doing the same thing until we release that fear.

We can remember the experience without holding onto the

pain and the emotions tied to the experience. Often, the emotions and judging are not positive things helping us in any lives; they take a lot of energy.

We all have an area where we store all of this energy; typically people store all of these experiences in their hips but you can store it anywhere.

* Where do you store most of your energy?
* What is the area of your body that you always feel the most tension, stress, and pain?

That is where you store all of your experiences.

We can access our experiences whenever we would like, but whatever you are dealing with when you explore this, it will be deep. You will find that whatever you are dealing with now, you also stored in your body from many lives to deal with later. Once you start letting go of what you are dealing with now, the other experiences will rise, and you can begin to let them go. You will find it will take a few letting go sessions to make peace with it and set it free. When you do the letting go you may feel like everything clicks into place or you may see a whirlwind image where all of this is connected and you will feel free.

How Karma Works

If I do something to you, it happens to me in this life. It happens instantly. If I make you feel bad, I instantly feel bad. It is that simple and if you do something and do not make amends for it, you will feel it across lifetimes with that person. Thus, why you can be doing a letting go session and pick up on stuff from other lives.

Sometimes you will become aware of energy you are storing from past lives and when you release it, you will feel the shift in this life and in that life because of it. Everything happens for a reason, there are no accidents.

You will notice when you make amends during your letting go sessions, that if you are carrying something from another experience, fixing it there has an immediate effect on this life. By letting that thing go that you are carrying from another life, it will affect that life and this life instantaneously. This happens because everything is happening at the same time and everything is connected.

An Individual Example

A driver cuts you off on the freeway forcing you to slam on your brakes. You immediately get mad and frustrated. You may even yell and gesture at the person in front of you, making you even angrier.

This car drives away and minutes later you are still mad and frustrated, perhaps you are still mad at this driver as you get home. Why?

Because we are all one, when you got mad and frustrated at the other driver, you also got mad at yourself. The other driver will feel this energy coming at them, but they will decide to interact with it or to give it back to you. Either way, everyone involved experiences the same thing. What you give to someone else, you also give to yourself.

A Group Example

When a natural disaster happens, it stops us all. We feel it. Even if we do not know anyone personally that has been affected by it, we sympathize, we watch the news, and we may even get involved and try to help.

It will consume us for a period of time until we have helped and feel we can move on or we are distracted by something else. Regardless of what we do, in that moment, we are affected by whatever has happened.

Remembering We Are Love, We Are One

Pay attention to your energy in your interactions. Know that you always have a choice how to respond, and how you respond has a direct effect on how you will feel.

* Are you doing a dance with someone? How can you return to love in this situation?
* Are you being objective? What can you do differently to create a more peaceful situation?
* Are you thinking about the consequence of what you do and what the effect will be on you and everyone else? Think big picture, as everything is all connected, like a

spider web.

Ways to Connect

Something you can always do that will have a good impact on everyone is to send love. This is visualized as the White Light. (See Sharing White Light with Others, page 112.)

You can also surrender a situation to light. Release whatever possible outcomes you would like to see and know that it will all work out perfectly. (See Surrendering a Situation to White Light, page 113.)

Visualize returning to the ball of light in a meditation. Feel the peace, love, and happiness. Know that it is real and whatever else you are feeling is simply the absence of the truth. Let it go!

As we are love, love will always conquer all. We are all one, so if you are feeling love and peace, I am as well.

8 - Tips to Balance Your Body, Mind, and Spirit

Here are some extra tips to use with the tools you have learned in this book. Try picking one section and practice working on it for a month.

Tips for the Body

Listen to, take care of, and appreciate your body. After all, it is telling you something for a reason. In this life experience, it is the only body you have. Cherish it!

Listen to Your Body

Your body is your compass. It is constantly guiding you; you just have to pay attention to what it is telling you.

If you feel an ache or pain, why is that happening?

What can you do to let the pain go and get back to a pain free body?

Perhaps there is letting go to do or your body is telling you that something is not working properly and it could use some medical help.

If your body tenses or your stomach hurts after you make a decision, what is your body telling you to do?

If your body is reacting to something you ate or drank, notice how your body reacts the next time you eat or drink this item. Maybe this is not something your body would like to have. Try to give your body things that will help it thrive. If your body is not using energy trying to figure out how to process food it does not want, you will have more physical energy for other things.

Overall, pay attention to what you are putting into your body and what you are doing to your body. Just because something feels good for a few minutes, does not mean it is going to keep feeling good.

For example:

When drinking a glass of wine, one glass is fine, two may be okay, but by time you are done with a bottle, it may not be such a good thing anymore. How much you drink determines how much time your body has to spend processing this and not putting as much energy into something else, like fighting off viruses.

Your body is constantly giving you clues and messages. Instead of just ignoring them or brushing them to the side, pay attention to them and see what happens.

Take Care of Your Body

Taking care of you is essential! If you do not take care of yourself, who will?

Think about the care you give yourself versus your children or others.

* Is it different or the same?
* What would you like to do to take better care of yourself?
* What is keeping you from doing it?

* How can you start taking better care of yourself? Remember; start with small little steps to help you reach your goal.

Every day you can choose to take care of yourself, and in doing so, you will be able to help others more effectively. It is like the oxygen mask on the airplane. You give yourself oxygen first so you can help others.

There are many ways to take care of yourself:

* Surround yourself with people that support and nurture you.
* Enjoy activities that relax as well as reenergize your body.
* Do mini meditations throughout the day. You can do this outside as you are walking, sitting on a bench, in nature, or even while relaxing in the bathtub.
* Exercise is important in caring for your body. What exercise will you do to support your body? How often will you do it?
* What food should I be giving my body? What is it telling me it would like?

It is different for each of us, so find what works best for you!

When you treat yourself with the same love and respect you show your loved ones, you are creating balance for yourself.

If you are in a good place, then you are in a good place to take care of those you help without throwing your body out of balance.

Appreciating Your Body

Your body is the only body you have in this life experience. Yet, we often ignore the parts we do not like to look at because others have told us these parts are not good (they judged our bodies and we accepted their judgment), we have hurt the parts and they are changed (perhaps in an accident or we have scars), or the parts have been hurt by someone else (either physically or verbally by being made fun of for your physical attributes at some point in your life).

If you are not appreciating all of your body, then chances are you are ignoring parts that would like to be healed. Sometimes pains are a sign of something that could be fixed, if you acknowledged it in a timely manner. It is important to be aware of your whole body and what it is telling you to do.

Mirror Exercise

This is an exercise to help you appreciate your entire body, every last hair, freckle, and wrinkle. Yes, wrinkles come from years of fun experiences and knowledge so we appreciate them too!

This exercise will also show you what the things are that you have to let go of so you can appreciate ALL of your body.

Stand in front of a mirror naked. Yes, completely naked. There is nothing to hide. You know all the secrets of your body, after all, you put them there.

Look at each part of your body. Start with the hair on the top of your head and say, "I appreciate _____."

As you look at each part of your body, you will appreciate it.

From the top of your head, go to:

* Your face
* Your neck
* Your shoulders
* Your chest
* Your stomach
* Your back
* Your butt
* Your hips
* Your genitals
* Your thighs
* Your knees
* Your shins
* Your calves
* Your feet

As you go to each area you say, "I appreciate _____." Imagine sending White Light to each part of your body as you approach it and appreciate it.

If you find you cannot appreciate something, ask yourself why.

* What is hiding there?
* What is preventing me from appreciating this part of my body?

Do one of the letting go exercises to help you let it go and appreciate that part of your body. You know the letting go is done when you can actually appreciate that part of your body.

You will always know why you are not appreciating a body part. If it is something you have buried deep and you are not comfortable processing that right now, that is okay. Instead, give that area White Light and smile at it. You can do that part next time; just make sure there is a next time.

For example: If you do not like how your stomach looks because it is full of stretch marks from having kids, then appreciate all the work your body went through to have the kids. Think of all the work your skin, muscles, heart, lungs, etc., did to help you have your beautiful children. Release the judgment and criticism, and replace it with love and appreciation. I appreciate that my body was able to have my beautiful children and I appreciate all the work my body did. I can see the work in my stretch marks and I appreciate them.

When you have gone from the top to the bottom of your body, literally, bring the White Light through your body. Then say:

"I am thankful for my body."

"I appreciate every cell and every part of my body."

"Thank you (Universe, God, etc.), for my body."

Do this exercise weekly until you are able to appreciate every single part of your body. Every part is there for a reason. Every part has a function in helping you be in this experience. Appreciate all of your body.

Tips for the Mind

The mind tells you what to think about and when. Often it helps you stay stuck in judgment, negativity, and thinking about worse case scenarios, but the mind can be helpful. It can help us find organization, filter out unnecessary stuff for us daily, and it can operate in a positive environment. It is all in how you use your brain.

This section has exercises to help you release judgment, go with the flow, and live in the present moment.

Release Judgment

There is no judgment of good or bad unless we put it on there, rather it simply is.

Everything that is happening is happening so we can experience it.

Things only become good or bad when we judge them to be so. Have you noticed that there is not one thing that every society can agree on being good or bad? It is because everything simply is.

Judging Yourself

Since everything happens for a reason, it is important to appreciate all of the experiences that we have had. When you find yourself judging and categorizing past experiences, stop and instead appreciate what you learned from it.

Sometimes you may have a glimpse of something that happened to you in another experience or life. If you are able to see those moments, ask yourself how that has shaped who you are in this experience instead of judging it. Is there something you are still carrying in your cells from that experience? Perhaps, something you can let go of from then, that will help you not only now, but at that time also.

Remember as you go about your day, if you start to judge yourself for your past experiences, stop that thought and instead focus on the good from that experience. If that does not work, always think about what you are grateful for in this moment.

Being Judged

You are not meant to know what others are thinking of you. If you find yourself judging yourself through someone else's eyes, just walk away. Be grateful for something in that moment instead.

Stop yourself every time your mind starts to wander back to that situation. For all you know, they were saying how fabulous you are and you let your imagination run off to the worst case scenario.

Every time your mind wanders back to this situation, stop it. "I am grateful for _____." Focus on this instead.

Judging Others

If you find yourself judging others, stop yourself. Remember, we are all one. If you judge someone, you will feel bad way longer than the minute you spent judging them. Think about a time where you judged someone and how you felt during and after?

Sometimes the ego lets us think that we are somehow better than someone else. No matter how intuitive you are, you cannot see the whole picture when something is happening. You can see pieces, possibly big chunks, but not the whole thing. Often it takes years to see the whole picture.

Remember, if you cannot see the whole picture at any given moment, how can you judge someone or something with a small piece of information? It simply is. Let it be. Instead, focus your mind on what you are grateful for in this moment. "I am grateful for _____."

Go with the Flow

In every moment you are either going with the flow or you are going against the flow.

Going with the flow means that you are going where opportunities are appearing that you could not see coming beforehand. It is not something that you create in your mind, rather, you may feel a pull to do something or say something, and this gets things rolling.

When you are going with the flow, you trust a higher process (God, the Universe, Love, whatever you choose to call it).

Often, you will know when you are going against the flow. Things will seem hard, they seem stagnant, no matter what you do or how hard you try to make something happen, it just is not working out. When you are in this place, there is always an easier way.

You have heard that saying, "When one door closes, another opens," or "When one door closes, a window opens," but what exactly does it mean? It means that when you are trying to do something and it just is not working out no matter how hard you try, perhaps there is another way. After all, when one door closes, a window opens somewhere, there is another way. The moment you let go of doing it "that way," a new way will appear.

Going with the Flow Exercise

Imagine that you are a leaf floating along the water in a stream.

If you are able to float effortlessly wherever the currents take you, that is going with the flow.

If you notice you are stuck, check in objectively and ask, "What else can I be doing?" Do it, and back you go along the stream.

Wherever the stream takes you, you go. You will find that things work out easily and almost effortlessly when you go with the flow.

Holding On

Holding on is what happens when your leaf lands on a rock in the stream and no matter how you try to get it back in the water, it stays stuck to the rock.

Perhaps you have it in your mind that to do something it must be done a certain way. Even though that way is not working anymore; you keep doing it over and over again. It is like you are banging your head on a wall. Energetically, you will feel stuck or frozen.

Notice that eventually (do not judge how much time it took you to realize this was not working), you give up. In that moment, by giving up the idea that it has to be done a certain way, you allow things to go with the flow and it works out perfectly. I am sure you can think of some examples where this has happened.

Holding on Versus Going with the Flow

One example of holding on versus going with the flow is vision boards. You make one, you hang it up, and you look at it every day. It seems like nothing on your vision board happens. You are holding on to what you think should happen and perhaps even how, when, and where it should happen. Often instead of course correcting, you hold onto how you thought it should work out, regardless of other possibilities around you. Instead of remembering that everything works out perfectly, you put a lot of energy into trying to make it work out your way. Chances are if it is not working out your way that is not the best way for you.

Going with the flow looks much different. You make a vision board and you put it away in the back of your closet. You forget about it, you stop trying to control how everything could possibly work out, and instead you trust that it will all work out perfectly.

You find it five years later, and when you look at it, you will see that you received a lot of things you put on the board. It may not look exactly like you thought at the time, but something even better than you originally envisioned happened. You still set out your intentions to the Universe, but then you released how, where, when, and why it should happen. When you are going with the flow, you trust the Universe to bring you opportunities; you just have to receive them.

When you go with the flow, things will work better than you could have imagined. You will also find things move faster and easier. You set an intention (what you would like), and then you release it (pay attention to the words you are using in your intention.) Not only have you told the Universe what you would like, but that you are open to better possibilities at the perfect time.

Everything we experience happens for a reason. If you do not get what you thought you wanted, it was not perfect for you, it was simply something you wanted. By going with the flow and holding open the space for the best thing to come to you, allows the best outcome.

* Where are you going with the flow in your life?
* What are some areas you could go more with the flow than you are currently?
* What will you do to go more with the flow?

Live in the Present Moment

Saying "I am" statements and being grateful for something in this moment help you live more in the present moment.

When you live in the present moment, time goes by slower than if you are not.

If you are focused on what is going to happen next or what happened in the past, the time literally flies by you. Now imagine the days becoming weeks, months, and so on. This is how time passes us by. If we are not enjoying it and going with the flow, it literally flies by.

Try to spend the days you do not have a tight schedule by going with the flow of the day. Spend this day not paying any attention to the clock. It is amazing how much time we spend checking the time instead of enjoying the time.

For example:

* Eat when your body is hungry. Really enjoy the smell, appearance, and taste of your food.
* Take a nap if you are tired. Let your body tell you when it is bedtime, not the clock.
* Catch up with a friend or family member that is special to you.
* Sit outside in nature and enjoy everything around you. Take in the beauty around you.
* Enjoy your shower or bath instead of rushing through it to get to the next thing.

Try it. Notice how much slower time goes by when you are not rushed and measuring how much can be done in a time period.

After you have spent a day living in the present moment, notice what happens when you go back to your vigorous, time watching schedule. How do you feel at the end of a day like this? Try to spend more time not following the clock on days and moments when you do not have to. You will really enjoy them.

Appreciate your surroundings, the people around you, be grateful. Being grateful is the most powerful way to live in the moment and really remember the moment. How can you live more in the moment? What will you do to implement this in your daily life?

Tips to Connect with Your Spirit

Connecting with your spirit is freeing. It releases you from the physical barriers we experience on this plane. This section has some tips to help you feel free and share with others at the same time.

Remember, it is very important to stay grounded. Always make sure you can feel the White Light going into your feet, and into the Earth. If you are not, you will feel out of balance and you will not be able to effectively help yourself or anyone else.

This section has tips to help you with abundance, sharing White Light, and surrendering a situation to White Light.

Abundance

The Universe is full of abundance; there is plenty of everything to go around for everyone.

It sounds simple and it is, but often we try to control what this abundance means instead of trusting that we will have exactly what we should at the perfect time.

In the beginning, you think you know what abundance it is that you would like to attract or bring into your life. Often, you spend time visualizing this, and focusing on this, and nothing else. However, as you do the Abundance Meditation and you see all of the abundance coming in and in ways that you did not imagine, you will realize that when you trust the Universe to allow whatever abundance you should be receiving in, everything flows at its best.

Abundance is more than money. It is also allowing in all the opportunities that the Universe is giving you. Relationships, experiences, love, food, and material items are just some of the opportunities around you in every moment. Often we do not allow every opportunity in and typically, abundance is focused on money, but it is so much more; do not limit yourself. Instead receive your abundance and be thankful.

If you put limitations on the abundance you receive, you are limiting yourself. The Universe does not put limits on us. It gives us exactly what we should have; we just have to accept it.

One day when you are letting abundance flow into your heart, you will find yourself saying, "That is enough, I do not need anymore." Please know, that the Universe is giving you abundance and for you to stop it is unnecessary. If you find yourself stopping the abundance, then ask yourself:

* What letting go is there for me to do in this area?
* What beliefs do you have about having money? Are they still working for you or are they preventing abundance in your life?

Then do the Abundance Meditation again and allow the Universe to let whatever abundance it is giving you in.

Abundance Meditation

Start by taking a few deep breaths.

Bring the White Light through your body. Imagine it entering your crown (top of your head), going down your face, your neck, to your chest and back, to your stomach, to your hips, to your thighs, to your knees, down your legs, into your feet, and into the Earth.

Hold your hands out like a V in front of your chest (as you do this more often, you can just visualize opening up your heart and keeping your hands at your side.)

Imagine allowing all the abundance to flow into your chest. Typically you will see pastel colors. Let them in. Sometimes you will see things like a stream, a bird soaring in the air, or some other nature scene. Go with whatever you see and where it takes you. See the beauty.

During your meditation you can also imagine masses of other people receiving their abundance and being happy.

Let the energy flow until you feel like it is finished. Fold your hands over your chest when you are done (like you are sealing the energy in). Thank the Universe for the experience you just had and for the experiences to come.

Receiving Abundance

Abundance will appear in many ways. New friends, better relationships with family members, opportunities will appear, and you will attract money. Money will come in many forms from finding coins on the street, to winning it, receiving it from unexpected sources, and even from deals and coupons.

Be aware of the abundance as you receive it and appreciate the abundance as it comes in to your life. Every time you receive abundance, say thank you to the Universe. This is a signal for the Universe to send you more because you liked it and appreciated it.

Keep doing your Abundance Meditation and you will notice the abundance keeps coming in. Stop doing it, and it instantly stops. When you start doing it again, abundance will start flowing again.

This really works! Do the meditation, be open to receiving what the Universe is giving you, and be grateful. There really is plenty for everyone.

Synchronicity, Miracles, and Coincidences

Is it a coincidence? Was it a miracle? Are they the same thing? How do they happen?

There is no such thing as a coincidence or a miracle because everything works out perfectly and everything works out exactly as it should. The Universe is putting things into motion all around us and there is a reason for each event. You can still call it a coincidence or a miracle, but know that it is not a mysterious event. It was supposed to happen and so it did.

Basically, this means that there are no accidents. You did not "bump" into someone at a coffee shop or at a store accidentally. You were supposed to bump into them. Sometimes you will know what that reason was when you see them; sometimes you will not because it was more for them than for you.

You will notice more coincidences or miracles when you are consciously paying attention to them. If you are focused on the text or email you just got and where you have to go next, you may not notice them at all. Then bigger things will happen to get your attention. Notice the small things, they add up and they mean something.

As you go through your day, pay attention to all the synchronicity happening around you and to you. Sometimes it is helpful to keep a log of your daily miracles in the beginning. You will notice that each day you notice more and more. Thank the

Universe for the opportunities it effortlessly provides you.

"I am thankful for this opportunity. I appreciate _____." This will attract even more of these opportunities to you.

Sharing White Light

Bringing the White Light through your body throughout your day helps you connect with your spirit and instantly calms your body. Once you start doing it daily for yourself, you will be ready to share it with others. You will see how it helps you and you can share it to help others as well.

It is very easy to share the White Light with other people, animals, plants, and basically anything that gives off energy. You can also surrender a situation to the White Light.

Sharing White Light with Others

Animals, babies, and little kids love White Light. Sometimes adults are less open to it at first. If someone does not take it or want it, that is okay. They are not ready for it.

You do not have to be near the person. You can send White Light to any person or thing anywhere. It only takes a moment to do it. Energy is not bound by our physical surroundings.

Start by bringing the White Light through your body. Imagine it entering your crown (top of your head), going down your face, your neck, to your chest and back, to your stomach, to your hips, to your thighs, to your knees, down your legs, into your feet, and into the Earth.

Then do the same thing (while you are still in White Light), to another person plant, or animal. Bring the White Light down from the sky, into whatever you would like to give the White Light to.

When you are finished, bring the White Light through your body again. Imagine it entering your crown (top of your head), going down your face, your neck, to your chest and back, to your stomach, to your hips, to your thighs, to your knees, down your legs, into your feet, and into the Earth.

Surrendering a Situation to White Light

When you have something "big" happening in your life, sometimes the best thing to do is to surrender the situation to the White Light. Whether it is a fight, a big change at work or in your family, or something very stressful to you, love conquers all. White Light is love.

When you surrender a situation to the White Light, things will work out better than you ever could have imagined. Think about how you feel in the White Light. It is calming, relaxing, and supportive. That is the best thing for any stressful situation.

Basically, you release the situation to the White Light, surround it and all the people involved in White Light, and say to yourself, "I surround the situation in light." Every time you think about it, imagine sending everyone and everything involved light.

Worrying about something does not solve or change anything.

It just attracts more of the same to you and that situation. However, if you release the situation, and send it White Light, you will attract that back to you, which in turn helps you be calmer and more relaxed about the whole situation.

Start by bringing the White Light through your body. Imagine it entering your crown (top of your head), going down your face, your neck, to your chest and back, to your stomach, to your hips, to your thighs, to your knees, down your legs, into your feet, and into the Earth.

Imagine the situation that is causing you stress. Take the situation and let it go, release it. You can imagine it floating up into the White Light or the sky.

Now, imagine everyone and everything involved in this situation. Surround them all in White Light. You can imagine wrapping the whole situation in a blanket of support and love too.

Bring the White Light through your body again. Imagine it entering your crown (top of your head), going down your face, your neck, to your chest and back, to your stomach, to your hips, to your thighs, to your knees, down your legs, into your feet, and into the Earth.

Every time you think about this situation, send it White Light (or love if that is easier for you to imagine). If you find yourself getting upset or tense, repeat this exercise. Do it every time you think about it until you feel at peace with the situation.

9 - As You Go on Your Journey

Everything Works Out in the Best Way Possible for Everyone Involved

Do not worry or stress yourself out about how something will work out. Instead know that every situation works out perfectly, not only for you but for everyone involved. When you find yourself worrying about an outcome, say, "Everything works out in the best way possible for everyone involved," and so it will be. You can also surround everyone involved in White Light.

Wherever You are Going, You Will Get There at the Perfect Time

If you find yourself running late, every time you catch yourself thinking you will be late, change that reality you are creating. Instead say, "I will get there at the perfect time." You will find when you say this, and believe it, that you are less stressed as you are trying to get to your destination and when you do arrive, that you did indeed arrive at the perfect time. Perhaps you will be on time, or they will be running late and you would have rushed there to wait anyhow. You will always get where you are going at the perfect time.

Life is a Glass of Milk

This is one of my favorite examples to share with clients about letting go.

Imagine your body is a clear glass. Chocolate milk is the negativity in your body. White milk is the White Light.

If your body is filled with stress, negativity, and all the emotions you stored during the day, week, or years, your milk is chocolate. It has the thick, chocolate liquid at the bottom. It is stuck along the sides of the glass and there may even be some chocolate floating on the surface. When your body is in this state, you can pour tons of white milk into your glass; however you will keep ending up with chocolate milk. After all, it is sticking to the glass, it is thick, and it is everywhere. The white milk may make the chocolate milk lighter, but it is still there no matter how much white milk you pour into the glass.

The solution is to dump out the chocolate milk by doing some letting go. While you are letting go you are able to clean the glass and remove all the chocolate liquid (negativity) in your body. You can also dry the glass and fill it with your "I am" statements. Now you are ready to pour the white milk into your glass.

Balance is Possible in Every Moment

What changes is what tool will help you find your balance in every situation. You will find that there are exercises in this book that you love to do and they will become your tool of choice. The ones that seem harder or more difficult may be the tools to help you when what you normally do is not working and in that moment you will love them.

I have used the tools in this book on myself, with my clients, friends, and family over the years. You have a good foundation for your journey. Tweak the tools and make them yours so they can help you in the best way for you. Just remember to always start with the White Light, in a place of love and support.

Now that you are aware of your energy and what throws you off balance, you will notice immediately when you start to get out of balance and that you do not like it. You will find that it gets easier to be in balance and that everything supports you in this state: your body, your mind, and your spirit.

Love is All There is

If it is not of love, it is not real.

"I am love. I am light. I am safe. I am whole. I am connected to the Universe." These are your truths.

Balance your energy from within. You have the tools!

The more free you feel, the freer you are. The more balanced you feel, the more balance you will attract around you. The more you trust, the more your life will unfold in ways you could not have planned. Everything works out in the best way possible, always.

About the Author

Lisa is the author of "Energy Balance: My Guide to Transformation," and has been working as an Intuitive Energy Coach for more than ten years. She was born with her intuitive abilities with energy healing, and is a Reiki Master.

She has the ability to see, sense, hear, and feel energy. Lisa knows why, where, and how each person stores energy within their body, how to release that energy, and how to reprogram that area with positive energy.

Lisa currently lives in San Diego, California with her family. For more information about Lisa and her workshops and events, visit www.lisagornall.com.

Follow Lisa on Facebook at facebook.com/lisamgornall and on Twitter @LisaMGornall.

Made in the USA
Columbia, SC
20 August 2017